The **Lib**
Too

D1558124

The **Library Marketing Toolkit**

Ned Potter

facet publishing

© Ned Potter 2012

Published by Facet Publishing
7 Ridgmount Street, London WC1E 7AE
www.facetpublishing.co.uk

Facet Publishing is wholly owned by CILIP: the Chartered Institute of
Library and Information Professionals.

British Library Cataloguing in Publication Data
· A catalogue record for this book is available from the British Library.

ISBN 978-1-85604-806-4

First published 2012

Text printed on FSC accredited material.

Typeset from author's files in 10/14 pt Palatino Linotype and Frutiger by
Flagholme Publishing Services.
Printed and made in Great Britain by MPG Books Group, UK.

For my incredible wife,
amazing parents,
and wonderful daughter

Contents

Acknowledgements

Huge thanks to Sarah Busby, formerly of Facet, for guiding me through the tricky process of writing a first book. Thanks to Andy Priestner for his strategic input, and Jodie Double for her digital insight. Thanks to Phil Bradley for his advice, to Terry Kendrick for his encouragement and to Stephen Abram for much inspiration. Thanks to my Dad for hours of proof-reading and advice, and a lifetime of support and encouragement . . .

Thanks to Antony Brewerton, whose time and input was vital in shaping the final version of this book.

Thanks to Mylee Joseph, Neil Infield, Samantha Halford, Mei Yau Kan and Joel Kerry, who all put me in touch with case study contributors.

Thanks to Twitter – without such a brilliant online network of support, suggestions, ideas and contacts, I would not have been able even to attempt this book! Thanks also to my employers, the University of York, for being brilliantly supportive.

Thanks to all the libraries who allowed me to use pictures of their marketing campaigns to illustrate these pages. Thanks to all the incredible case study contributors for giving their time and expertise.

And above all, thanks to my family.

Ned Potter

Introduction

The world of marketing is changing more rapidly than ever before, and libraries are having to change with it. While some are still stubbornly refusing to engage with the need to market themselves, or are doing so using techniques that pre-date the digital age, for the most part the industry is responding positively to the challenges of promoting our services. The first part of this introduction is an exploration of what marketing really is and why libraries need to do it innovatively and successfully; the intention is that the remainder of the volume will provide the tools and knowledge to achieve this, with case studies from people who have been there and done it well.

If the bad news is that libraries are still not always great marketers, the good news is that marketing has never been easier! Today's platforms and tools make it more straightforward, more direct and much cheaper than it ever has been before. Little changes in the library approach can yield big results.

About marketing

What is marketing?

Formal definitions of marketing tend to be rather severe – and, because most marketing is about promoting the sale of as many items as possible for as much money as possible, widely quoted definitions are often slightly wide of the mark when it comes to libraries.

What marketing is not, is simply a poster featuring details of a new database. That's advertising. It's not simply an online campaign about a new service, either: that's promotion. It's not an article in the newspaper about the head librarian: that's publicity (and if the article is about the librarian welcoming a famous celebrity to the library, that's PR). And what marketing *really* isn't, although visiting many libraries across the world might make you think otherwise, is an A4 piece of coloured paper with a promotional message about new books printed on it in Comic Sans font.

What marketing *is*, then, is an ongoing conversation with your target audience, which combines promotion, publicity, PR and advertising in an organized, strategic way. In fact, in the age of Web 2.0, you can probably get away without any traditional advertising if necessary. But the promotion, the publicity and the PR exist amid a constantly renewing and never-ending cycle of market research, planning, actions, follow-ups and evaluation.

Alison Circle, who provides a case study later in this book, describes it like this: 'Marketing is not a poster; marketing is understanding your customers and creating products and services for them – that only you can uniquely provide.'

Is it important to libraries?

There used to be a feeling that marketing was damaging the readers. And that is changing, now.

Terry Kendrick

Marketing is disingenuous. Marketing is polishing the truth. Marketing is outright lying. All of these statements can be true about marketing in general – but not about marketing libraries specifically. Without a doubt, marketing has in the past been something of a dirty word in our industry, considered a seedy or unseemly concept. I'm delighted to say these perceptions are shifting at last, and there are many information professionals plugged in to the need to market, and gaining an understanding of how to do it well. Sadly, part of the reason for this has been library closures – nothing makes clear the need to market successfully like a library being closed because it couldn't prove its value. Such are the times in which our profession currently strives to move forward.

Marketing a library is not like marketing a shampoo. Shampoo manufacturers push the limits of what they can say (sometimes too far, ultimately falling foul of advertising standards agencies . . .) about the astonishing properties of their product – be they regenerative, health-giving, or simply shine-enhancing. It's a hard sell, attempting to bedazzle the consumer into choosing them. Libraries are not operating on that level. We are not trying to dupe people into using our services, or stretch the truth about what we do to breaking point. Library marketing is *outreach*. It is making people aware of what we can do for them, in a language they can understand. It really is that simple – and that honest. We need to tell people we're here, explain to them how we can help, and persuade them to come in through the doors, physical or virtual.

Marketing is important to libraries because people need to be convinced of the need to use them. Public perception is at least ten years behind the reality of what we do and how we do it, and in any case there are now more ways to access information than ever before – many of the major technological advances in the last decade have focused exclusively on this area. The internet changed the world, and the internet is mostly about access to information of one sort or another.

Marketing is important because public libraries need more people in through their doors using more of their resources, because academic libraries need more students and staff to value the services they provide, because special libraries need the businesses they serve to value them. We all have to market in order to survive. 'Marketing as afterthought' is no longer a viable model for our future.

The other thing about marketing libraries is that it is fun. It's actually quite enjoyable! It is certainly infinitely do-able. Marketing becomes a mindset, and once you occupy that mindset it's easy to start making changes to your library's approach to promotion and to see results quickly. The tools and the audience come and go, but the mindset remains the same – and thinking like a library marketer need only involve remembering and acting upon a few key concepts, which are detailed in Chapter 1.

The next section of this Introduction gives you some more information about the book itself and how it can be used.

About this book

This book attempts to cover a huge territory – public libraries, academic libraries, special libraries, and special collections and archives. No single volume could completely document all there is to say on marketing libraries, so I've tried to prioritize the absolutely key areas and developments. This is a very practical book: the hope is that you can read the advice – particularly that which can be found in the case studies – and apply some or all of it to your own library and your own circumstances. You don't need the word 'Marketing' in your job title to be able to utilize the techniques and platforms described in these pages; we're all marketers now.

There is a website which works in conjunction with the book – this can be found at **www.librarymarketingtoolkit.com**. It contains lots of useful resources, including some guides and links for which there was not room here; additional case studies; and a blog which features up-to-date marketing tips and highlights best practice from around the information industry. At the end of each chapter in this book, you will find a link to a corresponding web page on the *Library Marketing Toolkit* site: they will contain further reading and related resources. These pages aren't listed on the menus of the website itself – they are bonus content, exclusively for readers of the book.

A quick word on language: the debate on whether we call the people who use our libraries 'patrons', 'users', 'members', 'customers' or some other term seems to be endless. There are arguments and counter-arguments for all of them; I've chosen 'users' for the most part in this volume, but where my contributors have used other terms these have been left as they were written.

Chapter summaries

This is a firmly 21st-century marketing text. There is a suite of three chapters all about various forms of marketing online, and the internet runs through the book like a vein. After all, chances are the majority of user interaction with the library is online in one form or other, rather than in person. Even libraries with a very high footfall will see that dwarfed by hits, page-views and followers. Despite all this, the book builds from the foundations of marketing upwards – which means covering the important concepts first, then the strategy, then the brand which informs everything the library does to market itself.

This section contains a brief synopsis of each chapter; the case studies and their contributors are listed in the next section, below.

Chapter 1: Seven key concepts for marketing libraries

This chapter introduces some important ideas which underpin the techniques and tools described in the rest of the book: in particular, the need to market benefits rather than features.

Chapter 2: Strategic marketing

Marketing is more successful when it happens as part of a constantly renewing cycle. The aim of this chapter is to demystify the process of strategic marketing, simplifying it into seven key stages with advice on how to implement each one. Particular emphasis is put on dividing your audience and potential audience into segments, and marketing different messages to each group.

Chapter 3: The library brand

A library's brand is the sum total of everyone else's perception of it – we can't control this, but we can attempt to influence it. The chapter looks at branding your library with a high quality visual identity, designing promotional materials, and even library merchandise.

Chapter 4: Marketing and the library building

Closely related to the previous chapter, this section looks at the design, layout and decor of the library and how this can influence the way it is used. There is also some insightful information on what tangible benefits are to be had from redesigning and refurbishing library premises.

Chapter 5: An introduction to online marketing

This chapter covers the fundamentals of online marketing: the library website (including Search Engine Optimization), its mobile version, library apps and successfully marketing with e-mail.

Chapter 6: Marketing with social media

The development of social media is arguably the most important thing to happen to marketing this century, and more and more libraries are making use of various platforms to talk directly to their audience. Your users and potential users *are* using tools like Facebook and Twitter, so this chapter gives step by step instructions on setting up library presences on these platforms, and then on taking them to the next level. It also covers blogs and Google+.

Chapter 7: Marketing with new technologies

There are plenty of new technologies which don't come under the umbrella of social media, but which still make for exciting marketing possibilities. This chapter contains advice on marketing with video, using image-sharing sites, deploying QR Codes and the new wave of location-aware mobile applications such as Foursquare.

Chapter 8: Marketing and people

This section covers collaborating with people and reaching people, including Word of Mouth Marketing, one of the single most important tools in the library toolkit. Other topics covered include reaching remote users, marketing to multicultural communities, elevator pitches and cross-promotion.

Chapter 9: Internal marketing

Internal stakeholders often hold the purse-strings to our libraries, so marketing successfully to them is absolutely essential. The first part of this chapter covers language, telling stories, using statistics, marketing upwards and communicating your message well. The second part covers marketing *with* internal stakeholders, such as a parent company within whose branding guidelines you must promote the library.

Chapter 10: Library advocacy as marketing

We are all library advocates now, as the industry and profession face difficult times. This chapter looks at how to utilize library advocacy in general to market your library in particular, and also covers the echo chamber problem and 'Trojan Horse advocacy'.

Chapter 11: Marketing special collections and archives

Many of the techniques and strategies described in the previous chapters apply equally to marketing special collections and archives, but these areas come with specific challenges of their own. Covered here are marketing digital collections, promoting ancient materials with modern methods, mounting displays and exhibitions, tapping into cultural events at a national level and harnessing the power of crowds to develop and market your collections. Some of these ideas and techniques are applicable across the board, so the chapter isn't designed to be read only by those working in special collections and archives.

Appendix: Glossary of Web 2.0 tools and platforms

A glossary explaining the terms used and platforms described in Chapter 6, 'Marketing with Social Media', in particular.

Case study matrix

The strength of this book lies in its 27 case studies, from the UK, the USA, Canada, Australia, New Zealand and Singapore. They feature institutions and individuals of outstanding calibre, who have applied the techniques they describe in the real world and had success with their libraries. My aim in the rest of the text is to provide a framework in which to allow the real experts to share their first-hand experiences.

Table 0.1 lists the case studies, the authors, which chapters they appear in, and some of the topics they cover. It also lists the sector with which the author is most readily identified, but in most cases the advice they give applies universally.

Brief biographies appear before each case study in the text itself. Links to the contributors' organizations and personal web pages can be found on the website (at **www.librarymarketingtoolkit.com/p/about-contributors.html**). Occasionally there will be quotes from contributors elsewhere in the book, outside of their case studies – if you spot an unreferenced quote, that's because it was given for this volume.

Table 0.1 *The case study matrix*				
	Case-study title	Author	Sector	Chapter	Key themes
1	Key issues in strategic marketing	Terry Kendrick (Consultant, UK)	All	Strategic marketing	Strategic marketing, the marketing plan, market research, quick-wins, segmentation
2	Gaining feedback from library users and non-users	Rebecca Jones (Consultant, Canada)	Special, Academic	Strategic marketing	Feedback, interviews, focus-groups, using data, reports
3	Measurement in marketing Columbus Metropolitan Library	Alison Circle (Columbus Metropolitan Library, USA)	Public	Strategic marketing	Customer behaviour, segmentation, strategic marketing, brand architecture, measurement, outputs and outcomes
4	Designing on a shoestring	Jessica Wykes (City University, UK)	Academic	The library brand	Design approach, sourcing and working with images, software, visual identity

continued on next page

Table 0.1 *Continued*

	Case-study title	Author	Sector	Chapter	Key themes
5	Sshhh...! bags and library merchandise	Katy Sidwell (University of Leeds Library, UK)	Academic	The library brand	Merchandise, aggressive marketing, brand building, stereotypes
6	Marketing a converged service	Stephen Pinfield (University of Nottingham Information Service, UK)	Academic	The library brand	Launching a converged service, marketing agility in large organizations, marketing services not concepts
7	Library design and visual merchandizing	Kevin Hennah (Consultant, Australia)	All	Marketing and the library building	Visual merchandizing, visual identity, branding, floor layout, library design principles
8	Redesign and refurbishment	Fiona Williams (York Explore, UK)	Public	Marketing and the library building	Rebranding, refurbishment, redesign, flexible spaces, security, impact
9	Seven essential elements to an awesome library website	David Lee King (Topeka and Shawnee Public Library, USA)	Public	An introduction to online marketing	Website, blogs, mobile, strategic plan, social media
10	Mobile options for library websites	Aaron Tay (National University of Singapore Library)	Academic	An introduction to online marketing	Mobile-ready websites, library apps
11	How to market with e-mail	Alison Wallbutton (Massey University Library, New Zealand)	Academic	An introduction to online marketing	Tone, visual feel, avoiding information overload, bringing together marketing channels through e-mail
12	Social media at the British Library's Business and IP Centre	Frances Taylor (British Library, UK)	Public, Special	Marketing with social media	Facebook, Twitter, LinkedIn, YouTube, social media marketing principles, user interaction, marketing mix
13	Twitter at NYPL	Kathy Saeed (New York Public Library, USA)	Public	Marketing with social media	Running Twitter with multiple contributors, replies and interaction, social media strategy
14	Facebook at Manchester Libraries	Sue Lawson (Manchester Libraries, UK)	Public	Marketing with social media	Facebook and engaging content, Facebook and wider social media activity
15	New frontiers and Web 2.0 tools	Aaron Tay (National University of Singapore Library)	Academic	Marketing with new technologies	Web 2.0 catalogues, live chat functionality, geolocational apps

Table 0.1 *Continued*

	Case-study title	Author	Sector	Chapter	Key themes
16	Using technology to market the library to teens	Justin Hoenke (Portland Public Library, USA)	Public	Marketing with new technologies	Engaging the youth demographic, audio technology, gaming and games
17	Engaging the local media in marketing the library	Rob Green (CILIP Update and Gazette)	Public, Academic	Marketing and people	Placing stories, working with journalists, press releases, utilizing the media
18	Marketing to multicultural communities	Oriana Acevedo (State Library of New South Wales, Australia)	Public	Marketing and people	Multi-cultural communities, the MyLanguage project, accessibility, integration
19	Marketing a remote library service on a budget	Joanna Wood (Children and Family Court Advisory and Support Service, UK)	Special	Marketing and people	E-mail and online promotion, library champions, reputation
20	Effective internal marketing and communications – ten rules of success	Rosemary Stamp (Stamp Consulting, UK)	All	Internal marketing	Delivering key messages, language, identifying audiences, response management
21	Marketing upwards	Andy Priestner (Cambridge University, UK)	Academic	Internal marketing	Marketing to senior managers, personalization, aligning with the mission, documenting success
22	Marketing within strict branding guidelines	Susan Moore (Institute of Chartered Accountants in England and Wales)	Special	Internal marketing	Marketing with a parent organization, engaging with professional marketers, segmentation
23	Advocacy and library marketing	Elizabeth Elford (British Library, Society of Chief Librarians)	Public	Library advocacy as marketing	National versus local profile, building relationships, benefiting from national campaigns
24	Five top tips for marketing an archive service	Lisa Jeskins (Mimas, Archives Hub, UK)	Archives	Marketing special collections and archives	Objective setting, key audiences, key messages, key channels, getting online
25	Digitization and the halo effect at TNA	Caroline Kimbell (The National Archives, UK)	Archives	Marketing special collections and archives	Digitization and access, tools for marketing archives, social media, licensing commercial images

continued on next page

Table 0.1 *Continued*				
	Case-study title	Author	Sector	Chapter	Key themes
26	The 100 Objects project	Alison Cullingford (University of Bradford Library)	Special Collect-ions	Marketing special collections and archives	Exhibitions, online campaigns, cultural landscape, marketing ancient materials with modern tools
27	Harnessing the crowd – marketing your library with crowdsourcing	Ben Showers (JISC, UK)	Special Collect-ions, Archives, Academic	Marketing special collections and archives	Crowdsourcing as a marketing opportunity for libraries, promoting crowdsourcing projects

Low cost marketing

The original version of this text had a whole chapter on marketing on a budget, until it was pointed out to me that more or less *all* the techniques described here are either very cheap to implement or actually free. They cost time rather than money, and if you're reading this then hopefully you're already of a mind that it's worth taking the time to ensure the library is being used as much as it should be, and is valued accordingly. A common theme that emerges from the case studies is that a lack of investment doesn't necessarily have to inhibit good marketing practice; in fact, it often inspires creative solutions.

Chapter 1 kicks things off by looking at some of the key concepts which inform the tools and methods described later in the book. Remember these, and you're already halfway there.

CHAPTER 1
Seven key concepts for marketing libraries

This brief chapter outlines seven key concepts for marketing libraries, which underpin all the more practical ideas and techniques that follow. Keeping these concepts in mind can help bridge the gap from where much library marketing is now, and where it needs to be for the industry to be able to flourish.

The seven concepts

1 Everyone is trying to get from A to B. We have to show them how we'll help get them there quickly and more successfully.

Everyone's on a journey to where they want to go – these days they don't have a lot of time to sit down to consider an offer from a marketer. They're running from A to B, head down. As a marketer you're going to find it difficult to stop them, turn them around to pay attention to your idea, listen to it and then understand what it means for them. Your best bet is to target messages at them which truly help them get to where they're already going and make it absolutely clear how the library helps them to do that. You cannot assume that users will understand what you are talking about and will immediately translate that into what it means for progressing their journey faster with it than without it. That's your job as a marketer, which of course means that you must truly understand the users and their journeys.

Terry Kendrick

To understand how to market libraries, it's essential to understand the mindset and circumstances of the people we're trying to market them to. This is true across all sectors. We all know that in today's age we're bombarded with information, images, messages, advertising, promotion: our daily lives are sound-tracked by the white noise of people or things trying to get our attention. As a result we run with our heads down, as Terry Kendrick says in the quote above, just trying to get where we want to go, while ignoring the information overload.

We can't expect people to break off from their A to B journey to come and chat to us about whatever product it is we're selling. We live in an age of targeted advertising and hyper-personalization – people are less inclined to investigate something on the off chance that it's useful, because they're used to bespoke suggestions and information coming direct to them. Plus, they're really keen just to get to B.

For libraries, this means we have to run alongside these people, allowing them to continue their journey without slowing down, and make it absolutely explicit how we can help them do whatever it is they're already doing, but better. 'Better' might mean quicker, more efficiently, more comprehensively, more cheaply, or many other things – the onus is on us as library marketers to deduce what each person's 'better' constitutes, and quickly and successfully explain to them how the library can help. It's not enough to be just *another* way of accomplishing something – in order to respond to what Stephen Abram (2011a) describes as the 'asynchronous and asymmetrical threats' libraries face, we have to offer a *better* way of accomplishing something.

2 Market the service, not the product; market the benefits, not the features

Increasingly, libraries are moving towards marketing services rather than products – and thank goodness for that. Books are available from myriad sources; specialized help in finding the right one is not. Just marketing the 'warehouse full of books' side of libraries is to massively undersell what we do and how we do it, and is to fail to offer something more convincing than the alternatives to which we lose users every day.

Telling people about content puts the onus on them to think about how they can integrate that content into their lives; many people simply don't have time to analyse what we're offering in that way. We should be showing them explicitly how we can help them so they need no imagination to understand it – and that comes from marketing services. Law Librarian Sara Batts (2011) once said that the difference between community and collaboration is that community is and collaboration does. So to paraphrase Sara, content *is*, services *do*. 'Doing' is more useful to people than 'being', so when you have a very short time in which to appeal to people with limited attention span, market to them what you can do.

Related to this, and perhaps even more critical, is marketing benefits, not features. I really can't stress this enough – every librarian with an interest in marketing will tell you the same thing, and I've heard it said umpteen times at conferences, but libraries are, for whatever reason, hugely focused on processes. The rest of the world is focused on results. When marketing a service we should concentrate on *what people aspire to*, not the tools which will get them there. A classic example is databases: we often say things like 'we subscribe to 30 databases which you can access via the library catalogue'. We market the features; what people want to know about is the benefits. As library consultant Mary Ellen Bates says (2011), the way to market databases is to say 'we provide you with information *Google cannot find*'. This, after all, is where their value to the user lies – this is why they need the library, so they don't have to pay to subscribe to these databases for themselves. They don't care about the how. They care about the result: the information they need, unavailable elsewhere.

Marketing benefits rather than features doesn't cost a dime. It doesn't take any skill or imagination. It's just the approach – the way promotional materials are worded – that needs to change. If you run a course called 'Developing Information Literacy' you might get a few attendees; if you run a course called 'Finding high-quality credible information online, quickly and easily' you'll get a lot more. The first title is the feature, the second the benefit.

3 Market what THEY value, but continue to do what WE value

Perhaps one of the reasons information professionals can be suspicious of marketing per se is the idea that it will lead to libraries which are so focused on all the new-fangled cafés, e-book readers and free Wi-Fi, that they lose sight of their core mission to deliver the printed word. However, in actuality, we as a library industry can continue to do what we value, but we can put our promotional efforts into marketing what users and potential users value. The latter does not have to negate or contradict the former.

The Special Libraries Association in the USA ran a very important investigation, the Alignment Project, in order to ' . . . generate a sharper focus on the perceived value of the profession' (SLA, 2011). Key to the project was looking at the differences between how we as library professionals perceived the value of our services, and how those users and customers we served perceived the value of those same services. A survey asked providers (us) and users (them) what they most valued about information roles, and the results were revealing. 'Providing competitive intelligence' for example, scored more highly among the users – 22% saw that as being most valuable, compared with only 18% of providers. 'Managing the physical library' on the other hand saw a huge discrepancy the other way: 28% of providers saw it as most valuable compared to just 8% of the users. This is insightful information and, as the SLA concluded, it 'supports the need to emphasize more value-driven attributes rather than functional attributes' – but for the purposes of this section the message is this: we should continue to manage the physical library because, clearly, that's fairly essential; but we should focus our promotional efforts on things like competitive intelligence, because that's what the users value. We don't look at the results and instantly decide to close the physical space we call the library; we just adjust how we market our services.

The marathon runner analogy

Here is an analogy which ties together these concepts. In long-distance running events you'll often see refreshment areas, usually consisting of tables filled with cups of water or juice, and people holding them out for the runners to grab as they go past.

At the moment, libraries are manning one of those tables, full of lots of really good juice. What we tend to do is shout out at the runners that we have juice, it's right here, and that it is full of vitamins, and that vitamins are good for you, so why not have one of our drinks? We're competing with the other refreshment tables, and hoping for the best.

Now let's look at where we *need* to be. To market successfully, in this analogy we need a tray of juice that we take out to the runners. We have to run with them (as they go from A to B), tell them we can refresh them (market our services), and emphasize that we can help them run faster and longer (emphasize the benefits rather than explaining all about the vitamins . . .).

4 Market personality

People are fundamental to the marketing process. People do the marketing and it is at people that the marketing is ultimately aimed. More than that, though, libraries should market *their own* people.

People and personality are what separates libraries from the other myriad ways to find and obtain information these days. We literally add the value. This will become increasingly important as technology becomes more prevalent: the key thing about the new ways in which people access information is not the technology itself but the way we represent *our roles* as information professionals within the context of that technology. We can make sense of new technology for our users and help them integrate it into their daily lives; we know that our value lies in our expertise, but our approach to marketing seldom reflects that. We're still just promoting books and databases most of the time.

So, if we position ourselves as experts in new trends and technologies per se (rather than just, for example, gurus in a certain area such as geolocational apps), then when the technology goes mainstream, people will know to come to us for help and further information. It's not about saying 'Hey, the library is an expert in Foursquare!' – it's about saying 'The *librarians* know about new trends and technologies, come to us and we'll guide you through it!' and then when Foursquare (or anything else) goes mainstream, our users and customers already have us in mind as potential experts.

On the subject of personality, I would add that a personality trait that people generally find unattractive is insulting others to try and make oneself look good. Librarians have a tendency to insult Google as a means of promoting their own expertise or the value of libraries – for me, this is counterproductive and absolutely the wrong way to go about things. People switch off when you denigrate a tool that they use successfully every day, and as a result it's hard to win them round from the very start. People love Google. The 'librarian versus Google' war is not one we're ever likely to win, and it's one in which very few non-librarians are on our side. Even where our arguments are valid, Google is so powerful and all-pervasive that our views are very unlikely to stick in the public consciousness.

By all means *advise* people in the library on how Bing can be a better search engine in some scenarios. Go ahead and promote our search skills, which certainly trump those of an algorithm. Certainly flag up the fact that we have access to sources of information that Google does not. But market what we do well without resorting to abusing everyone's favourite search engine: if we have to mention Google in our promotional activities at all, it should be to market the fact that we can help people use it more successfully.

5 Never ever market something you can't deliver

It is absolutely essential to deliver on what you promise. Part of the marketing process is to tempt people to use your library's services, but marketing continues once they're through the door – and it extends to making sure that people get the service they expect from your promotion. Often during this book I'll be talking about the 'offer': the service or materials whose value to the user you are trying to articulate through marketing. When the marketing works and the user comes to claim the offer, that offer had better be there. A poorly delivered service that doesn't live up to the marketing claims will cause more harm than not having marketed it in the first place.

A promotional campaign should only ever be launched if there are resources in place to ensure that if the promotion works and people come or return to the library, they'll be so impressed they'll want to do so again.

6 Create and market different value propositions for different groups

We'll be talking about this in detail in the Segmentation section of Chapter 2 'Strategic Marketing', but it's worth flagging up here as an absolutely key concept of marketing libraries. One size no longer fits all.

We have expanded our offer from, essentially, just books, to all manner of other things – from children's activities, to cafés, to concerts – because of feedback from our customers. The important thing is to make sure we present different value propositions – different offers – for different groups of people. So we market the books to those who care most about the books, and we market the library as space to those who care about the library as space. Even the most product-oriented library, which still only really offers the printed word, can at least promote different variants of this to different groups of users and potential users.

7 Understand the cost curve, and how it applies to libraries

The term 'cost curve' hails from economics – it's a graph used to calculate the scale on which to produce an item or range of items in order to maximize profit. For libraries, of course, that original definition doesn't apply – instead, the 'cost curve' refers to the value your users get out of using a service you offer versus the cost of the effort they must put into doing so. The value must exceed the cost, and the fact that it does so must be made explicitly clear by us marketers, in order for the user to want to engage.

This seems really obvious, but think about how often libraries find themselves offering services that fall on the wrong side of the curve. For instance: you can access this database (offering great value to the user who wants the information it contains) but you'll need to log-in and follow these complicated instructions (which costs so much time and hassle it outweighs the value). From the very basics (signing up for a library card at all) to the new-fangled (scanning a QR Code to access unique library content) we must always be aware of how what we're offering is perceived, in terms of not just its value but its 'cost' to the user. The world is so used to libraries being 'free' to the user in monetary terms that this has almost ceased to be a selling point. We must focus on other value, and other cost.

As we shall see in the next chapter, 'Strategic Marketing', libraries are facing competition from all sorts of angles, so we must assess how our offer stands up to this competition. What are the alternatives to the cost of using your library, and is the value better? Something as mundane as literally 'doing nothing' is competition for the library – clearly the value isn't up to much, but the cost is tiny or non-existent, so 'doing nothing' may fall on the right side of the cost curve for many potential users. We have to entice them with a *better* offer.

Anchoring these ideas in marketing theory

This book doesn't contain too much theory or 'marketing speak', because that's been covered well elsewhere and I don't want people to switch off and be prevented from engaging with the real issues. The whole point of the book is to inspire *action*. However, one concept that is worth mentioning is Booms and Bitner's Seven Ps marketing model, because it ties together all of the above, and most of what follows in the book.

You may have heard of 'the four Ps of Marketing' – this refers to Product, Price, Placement and Promotion. Booms and Bitner (1981) sought to expand these specifically for service industries (like ours), and added a further three Ps: Participants (by which they essentially mean people), Process and Physical Evidence. Let's look at each of these and see how they apply to libraries.

1 **Product** refers to what we offer our users: books, journals, activities,

education, advice, professional expertise, searching, competitive intelligence, somewhere safe to go after school – whatever it may be. Product-oriented organizations are characterized by the fact that they produce a product based on what they think is right for the customer. Market-oriented organizations, on the other hand, base their product on feedback from the customers in terms of their wants and needs. In these changing times, it's hard to survive if you're solely product-oriented, and generally speaking I think libraries are doing their best to morph from product- to market-orientation. As stated in Concept 6 above, part of successful marketing is offering the appropriate product to different groups or segments.

2 **Price** traditionally refers to what people pay for the product, but of course in most cases libraries are free to the user. This is great for them, but not always so great for the library: people value things they have to pay for more highly than those they don't, even if the two things are more or less the same. In essence, it is easy to take libraries for granted. For our industry, the price we are asking people to pay is the Opportunity Cost (Concept 7) – we need to deliver a service that is compelling enough for people to spend their valuable time with us, if not their money.

3 **Placement** (or just 'place') refers to where and how the product is delivered and promoted. In libraries' case this often means the internet – and often we don't shout loudly enough about the fact that it is indeed we, the libraries, who have placed the products there. When users access electronic resources online, they often have no idea that the library has paid thousands of pounds to subscribe to these on the users' behalf. If possible, brand electronic content or provide a gateway which explicitly states: 'Provided by the Library'.

Place also refers to the location of the library or the service (as opposed to the decor and layout of the library, which is covered in Physical Evidence, below). Clearly in most cases the whereabouts of the library building is quite literally set in stone, and not something a marketer can hope to influence. However, we can take the service *to* the user in a lot of cases – whether that is by using Skype to develop a fuller relationship with a client in the special libraries environment, or setting up an outpost of the university library in the student's union building (for which all you need is a laptop and a sign that says 'Library'). Remember Concept 1 above – everyone is on their path from A to B. The services we provide need to be on that path, even if the library itself is not.

4 **Promotion** is the way in which we communicate what it is we do for our users and potential users. Once you get past Chapter 2, this book is *full* of promotion. Branding, visual identity, social media, the website, the way the books are displayed: it's all promotion. The best promotion is a two-way conversation rather than a one-way broadcast, which is partly why Web 2.0 tools are such a great opportunity for libraries.

5 **Participants** refers to the people, and addresses the main flaw in the original 'Four Ps' model. The people are both the users and the staff – customers often associate a product or service very strongly with the person who provided it. That is partly why Concept 4 is so important – marketing personality is essential.

6 **Process** refers to actually giving the service, and the way in which users experience it. Phoning the library up and being put on hold is a process with negative connotations; being able to return books at your local branch even if you took them out from the main branch is a process with positive connotations. Perhaps the most important message about process, however, as mentioned in Concepts 2 and 3 above, is that we care a LOT about it but users don't always need it described to them. They care about how well processes work, not what they involve at a library level. The reason this message features so heavily in this chapter is that marketing benefits rather than features is perhaps the single most effective change a library can make in its promotion, in terms of the time and expense of doing so (minimal) versus the impact it can have (huge).

7 **Physical Evidence** refers to the environment in which the product is delivered – in our case, the library building itself. This is covered in detail in Chapter 4 because it is so important in what we do. As Rafiq and Ahmed (1995) state, 'The physical environment itself (i.e. the buildings, decor, furnishings, layout, etc.) is instrumental in customers' assessment of the quality and level of service they can expect . . .'

For further reading on marketing theory, have a look at this chapter's associated web page: **www.librarymarketingtoolkit.com/p/7-key-concepts.html**. With the seven key concepts in mind, backed up by the theory of the Seven Ps, we'll begin to get more practical by looking at the strategic marketing cycle.

CHAPTER 2
Strategic marketing

Does your organization have a marketing strategy? If so, you're already way ahead of a lot of libraries. As an industry we're getting better and better at promotion, but promotional activities are only one aspect of marketing. Market research, segmentation, measurement and evaluation are all absolutely essential parts of the process, without which you have a series of unrelated promotions rather than a true marketing plan. These unrelated promotions can work well, but strategic marketing works *better*.

The marketing cycle

Real marketing happens in a cycle which constantly repeats. The goal of the marketing strategy is to ensure each part of this cycle is planned properly, and addressed properly. It's all about coming up with a plan that knits together all your activities, links them to wider strategic goals, allows you to analyse what works and what doesn't and improve things on an ongoing basis. The aim of this chapter is to demystify this process and make it as obtainable as possible for the modern, real-world library.

If you run a Google Image Search for 'marketing cycle' you get more than 22 million results. Clearly, then, there are plenty of models out there to choose from. Many are so complicated as to obfuscate their meaning for all but the most hardened marketing professional, and I don't want to put anyone off attempting strategic marketing. With that in mind, Figure 2.1 shows a diagram of the marketing cycle, as it applies to libraries, made as simple as possible.

As you can see, the promotional activities are around halfway through the process – if you start with promotion you've skipped a vital part (market planning), and if you stop with promotion you're missing another vital part (measurement and evaluation). This diagram is important because it

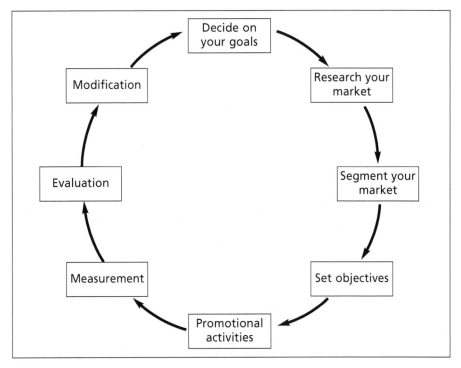

Figure 2.1 *The marketing cycle*

illustrates the cyclical nature of what we are attempting to do, and where the stages fit chronologically. I'm going to explain each of those stages in detail, and that will form the basis of this chapter; at the end, there will be an outline of a marketing plan to show how these fit together.

There are three case studies in this chapter: Rebecca Jones provides guidance on getting feedback from users, Alison Circle gives an expert view on measuring marketing activities, and first of all Terry Kendrick covers all aspects of marketing strategy and why it's important.

Case study 1: Key issues in strategic marketing | Terry Kendrick

Terry Kendrick is the guru of strategic marketing in libraries. His book Developing Strategic Marketing Plans That Really Work *(2006) is a must-read, and he writes, speaks, and runs workshops on marketing libraries all over the UK and in no less than 26 other countries. He also brings a non-library perspective to the table, lecturing in Marketing at the University of East Anglia.*

As a way of framing the specifics discussed in this chapter, I talked to him about all things marketing strategy.

Do you think that strategic marketing is undervalued in libraries generally?

I do. I think strategy setting is very well respected, I think libraries are very good at writing strategy documents – and I think they're actually quite reasonable at doing tactical programmes. The problem is that the strategic marketing planning part within those programmes isn't always so well bought into, because it's hard and it requires a lot of resources which aren't always readily available.

What are the consequences of marketing as afterthought? As in, the differences between making marketing a priority versus libraries who just do marketing if they get a chance once they've done everything else?

I think many libraries are driven by a series of pump-priming initiatives – so I think very few libraries use a full marketing approach. Many libraries feel the need to market what they've done as an initiative and then they're quite often disappointed by it because it's been done as a series of one-off activities without the coherence of a marketing plan. Is there evidence that marketing makes a difference? What I see in North America, in Canada in particular, where they're more marketing driven, is that it does make a real difference.

Is the first step to creating a marketing strategy understanding your own library or understanding the market your library is in?

I think the first step in creating any marketing plan is knowing what your ambition is. If you don't know what you want to be, the market doesn't matter and your capabilities don't matter either. I think it's very important to know what you want to look like, what you want to be – putting some numbers on that will focus the mind immediately. If you say you want to grow 30% over the next *x* number of years, that'll certainly focus your mind on the marketing: where in the market will that 30% come from, which users will give us issues, visits, enquiries, database hits – whatever it is driving the performance measures in that organization.

There is a difficulty using numbers, though, because I think perhaps libraries aren't used to planning like that – they find that quite intimidating. I think they want to do the promotional side of things rather than the harder side of the thinking – I think they're very good at DOING things, and it feels good to DO something, but to think your way through something is hard work, it can cause discord. And because there's not a culture of connecting marketing with the strategic planning those numbers which should be used as part of the marketing plan are seen as irrelevant to that process – when in fact they're very important.

Tell me about the importance of the library brand fitting into the user's lifestyle.
For most of the things we want to be associated with, we've got to feel good about them. We've got to feel that if we're seen there, then we're seen as 'okay' by the people whose opinions we value. People tend to have tribes and lifestyles and they live their lives in particular ways – it's not always the case that a library fits closely to that. If you have a lifestyle that, for instance, is fairly relaxed, you might want the library to be relaxed. The trouble is other lifestyles might not be quite as relaxed so there'll be a tension there in the way you market your service, which is very difficult to do. Good marketers can deal with that – they can market to different user groups with different lifestyles, simultaneously. Libraries don't always understand the lifecycle of their users – what they're doing in their lives.

Are any aspects of marketing strategy true across the board, or should everything be 'on spec'?
There are a few key concepts. One of them is that every library should be looking at the value it can offer its users in the way they live their lives, the journeys that they're on during their busy days, and how it helps them get there. There's no point in having (and talking about) resources when there is little value in the resource – the value only appears when the resource is in use. If you draw attention to the resource without explaining the outcomes that come from using that resource, you're actually setting yourself up to be cut because the danger with that is suddenly you draw attention to a pile of money being spent (for example on databases).

All libraries need to look at their value. The other thing that is key is not everyone perceives the same value in library services. So for every library doing marketing, it's key to undertake segmentation. Because it's the differences that matter rather than the similarities. It's no good looking for the one true way – but if you look at the value each segment attaches to the library, you've got the core of what marketing is about. Your planning should be driven by segments rather than the library as a whole, with an over-arching strategy for the library. What brings in the business and activity is the segments.

How do we ensure marketing is ongoing?
As libraries follow certain initiatives (rather than whole-service planning) quite often lots of activities will happen which are unconnected. It's really important, structurally, to have somebody whose responsibility it is to look at the activities

and find synergies to build on, particularly given that we know that one-off marketing activities will tend to be disappointing in their rate of response. Real results come from a certain amount of 'touches' to a particular user group over a period of time. It's really important that somebody is overseeing this. They don't have to be called a marketing specialist – marketing works best when it's an *orientation* for the library as a whole.

The worst thing that can happen is that if we send out some marketing which is successful, then people respond and come in to claim the 'offer' we're giving them and they're met with a poor response – that does more than just negate the activity you've just done, it positively reinforces the library as something which sends you irrelevant messages or makes promises it can't deliver. So that next time they receive a message from the library their first thought is 'last time I received a message they made an offer they didn't deliver on' not 'let's open this lovely message from the library . . .'

Understanding the market is a key part of the process.
Yes – any activities a library does or any service it offers, it's unlikely these days that we'll be the only people offering the service that people want. It's really important when you make an offer to your patrons that you understand what other things will be in their minds, what other offers are they being made which are similar, what other ways of achieving the same things will people have. Sometimes there'll be obvious other ways like Google, sometimes it's less obvious – it may be a friend they know who can help them with the same thing, or a strong competitor might be literally doing nothing, as in: why bother? It's important to understand what our offer looks like compared with competing offers. If we don't know that, we're likely to think that just marketing something will make it attractive. But who else is there, who are our rivals?

Can we make more of marketing the librarians rather than the library?
The more we can make the service look personal the better. An easy and quick way of doing this is to put pictures of librarians online and on promotional activity! I can understand the reluctance to do this, but we are, after all, a service not a product. Services are created by people, and they depend on how well people respond. Products are the same wherever you get them from. Services are different – people have skills, which is what makes us different from an information resource. Provided we have high quality skills, it's better to promote the people who deliver the service than it is to promote the products themselves – it's the people that add the value to the information.

Any tips for quick wins in library marketing?
Some of the quick wins in marketing are based around the key areas of segmentation and value. Many marketing activities will take quite a while to build up – if you try and look at the whole service at once you'll probably find the set of offers you have are either not strong enough or you won't have enough resources to fully implement them. So it's best to choose one group of people who you fully understand in terms of what they value, how they use your resources, what their outcomes are – take that segment and take it through a whole marketing planning cycle. It should be more manageable and should have impact relatively quickly – and everyone knows nothing succeeds like success. People don't want to necessarily do a large amount of marketing – those who don't, need to see those quick wins. There's a phrase about how you can lead a horse to water but you can't make it drink; the real trick is to make the horse thirsty *then* take it to the water . . . To make people thirsty for marketing within your organization, you have to show them quick wins – because in these difficult times no one wants to work hard on something which won't bear fruit for three to five years; there are a lot of benefits in the long-term view, but it takes a lot of nerve just to wait for them! So you need the quick wins to help get you there.

People always buy into marketing libraries – they really want to do it. But they go away . . . and it just doesn't happen. Six months later they've written a big document outlining everything, but the priorities have shifted. Advocacy and marketing – they've got to be bed-fellows haven't they? What a marketing plan does is make sure the offer the advocates make is actually there if the advocacy works!

It's an important time because if you look around the world, libraries are being cut all over. It feels like something bigger is happening – not just in libraries. We have to be careful because it could be that the last 30 years of libraries not biting the bullet on marketing is going to finally cost us.

Now we'll look at each stage of the marketing cycle individually.

1 Decide on your goals

In essence, this stage is all about asking the question 'Where do you want to be?' It is important to know what you want to achieve as a library (your 'mission') and design the marketing strategy to help achieve that. This helps embed marketing within the wider culture of the organization, and increases the likelihood of your being backed with meaningful resources.

Marketing can achieve many goals. It could be that you simply want more people through the doors; that would appear to be the most obvious motivation to market your library. But there's more to it than that: are you trying to attract new users, or increase the frequency with which the existing users visit? You may also wish people to use more (or particular) resources once they're there. You may wish to increase the library's reputation within the community (or even within the information profession, in order to attract the best staff). For archives and special collections, the aim can sometimes be to *decrease* footfall in order to protect the physical originals, by marketing their digital surrogates.

For all types of library, perhaps the ultimate goal is to ensure we are the first thing that comes to mind when people need the services we provide. Whether it's an information need (most likely), or a community need, or a training need – people must know we can provide it, and be convinced we can provide it better than anyone else.

Be brave with your goals. So many great ideas get bottlenecked by trying not to upset people; we are at a time when we need to inspire people, not protect their delicate sensibilities. Merely not failing is no longer enough. Think about how much of an impact a marketing campaign has to have on you personally in order to get you to try something new, and adjust your ambitions accordingly – because this is what we marketers should be aiming for, to *inspire* library use.

2 Market research

There are two main aspects to market research. The first is analysing the market within which your library sits. The second is analysing yourself: asking, where are we now? Once you know where you are, you can start to formulate a strategy for getting to where you want to be. Both stages are summarized by Terry Kendrick's quote above, 'It's important to understand what our offer looks like compared with competing offers.'

Analysing the market

Analysing the market involves several factors – in particular, exploring the community and demographics surrounding your library, analysing the competition which also serves these demographics, and looking inwards at your own services and existing offer.

For academic and special libraries with captive audiences, it is easy (and instructive) to calculate your market share. The market share is the percentage of an available demographic who actually use your services – so in the academic example, if 10,000 students have taken a book out or used an e-Resource in the last 12 months, and your total student body is 30,000, your market share equates to 33%. Once you have that figure, it's not a giant leap to setting a target for what you'd like your market share to be in another year's time, and then to set about deciding where your gains are going to come from and how you're going to get them.

Before going out and finding your own information about your community, make the most of existing data. Of course the library may have conducted market research in the past which could still be relevant, but beyond that there may be demographic reports from local government, national surveys of students at universities, or company reports for business libraries. With all of these the aim should be to identify groups of users and get to know them properly: identifying what their needs are, and identifying whether or not the library is currently meeting those needs. This is the beginnings of segmentation, and only after this stage can you really begin to market to the people involved.

However, within reason, existing users will continue to use the library regardless of the strategic marketing initiatives you employ – given that, analysing the market should focus primarily on finding out about *non-users*. How many potential users are out there, and how can you win them over?

Now we'll move onto the second part of analysing your market – you've explored your demographic, so now you must ask: who are your competitors? It's helpful to actually draw up a list and consider for each one what the library can do better than they can: if the answer is 'nothing' then your resources may be better invested in other areas. The library's competition includes *anything* the user could do instead of visiting the library or using its online resources. So whilst this covers the obvious competitors such as the internet in general (in particular Amazon for materials, and search engines for information) and bookshops, even things like 'doing nothing' are vying for our users' time.

Competitive benchmarking is a really useful way of analysing the market. It involves creating a list of user requirements, rating how you deliver services to meet these compared with your competitors' and, crucially, rating how *important* each of these requirements is to the user. Delivering the least important requirement much better than any of your competitors may not be enough. For example, the library used to be the go-to place for information, and now it has been usurped by the internet. Librarians often cite the unreliability of information found online as a reason to continue using libraries instead, but the fact is a lot of people don't actually *need* good quality information from highly respected sources. For many, basic information found via Google and Wikipedia is perfectly sufficient. This isn't true across all demographics, but it is true across some – the key thing is to only market 'providers of good-quality information' to those that value it.

Analysing yourself

Now you have defined the market, you can seek to define your library's place within it. By this stage you've already decided on your goals; you know what your ambition is and later you'll decide exactly how to achieve it. For now the task is to look at what you do well and what you do less well, see where your existing users are coming from and identify areas for growth – what can you offer potential new users?

Good feedback really is worth going the extra mile for, because it means that next time you change an existing service or introduce a new one, you're doing so in the *knowledge* that it's what people need, rather than the *hope* that it will be useful. This is a tricky area, however: feedback obtained through traditional channels is very rarely the unfiltered truth. On the one hand people may just tell you what you want to hear, out of a (misguided) sense of kindness because they think this will help you with your survey; on the other hand the people who do speak from the heart don't necessarily know what they *actually* want. It's always worth keeping in mind the famous quote from carmaker Henry T. Ford: 'If I had asked people what they wanted, they would have said faster horses.'

As a general rule of thumb, regardless of whether you obtain your feedback via surveys, interviews or focus groups, always take the opportunity to ask the respondents for their e-mail address and whether they would mind being contacted in future for further feedback sessions. A database of willing participants is a very useful thing to have, and it's also worth bearing in mind that data protection laws may mean that even if you have lots of your users' e-mail addresses already, you can't use them to solicit feedback on the library, or indeed market to them in any way, without their express permission. In the UK the rule is described like this: 'Personal data shall be obtained only for one or more specified and lawful purposes, and shall not be further processed in any manner incompatible with that purpose or those purposes.' (Information Commissioner's Office, 2011).

Feedback can be obtained in various ways once the various issues and pitfalls have been taken into consideration, and we'll look at three of them here – because good feedback is worth the investment.

Surveys

People are so fatigued by being surveyed these days; it takes something a little different to get meaningful feedback with this method. To create a long and traditional survey is to make the decision that you're prioritizing good-quality feedback over number of responses – that might be exactly what you need, of course, but it is often a law of diminishing returns as more and more potential targets develop *ennui* about the whole process over time.

To entice a high amount of respondents you may need to do something shorter and snappier. Here are some tips:

1 Only ever ask questions which will give you *actionable* results. In other words, don't ask people what they think about the look of the building if you have neither plans nor budget to change this if they all hate it. Save space by cutting out everything you can't practically respond to in the near future.
2 Rather than one massive annual survey which everyone dreads and which takes months to process and analyse afterwards, why not try a monthly 'Two-minute poll' which addresses just one or two key issues each time?
3 Traditionally, incentives go to survey respondents. However, at the London School of Economics they often offer incentives to the member of staff who can generate the most responses to a poll – this competitive element always guarantees a good return.
4 For larger surveys, offer a potential reward that respondents actually *want*. A £10 or $10 book token is exactly that: a token gesture. If you're going to offer an incentive at all, it has to be something that will persuade people to take part in the survey *who otherwise wouldn't bother*. An informal poll among librarians of my acquaintance suggests a prize-draw for an iPod significantly boosts responses – an iPod Nano is really very cheap to purchase as a prize if, as a result, you get a larger body of data about your library with which to inform key strategic decisions.

5 If the survey is online, try and keep the number of screens/pages to an absolute minimum. You don't need a welcome screen, an explanation screen, then different screens introducing each section. Ideally, the link you give your users to access the survey should contain all the questions, right there and then.

6 Finally, tell the participant right at the start how long the survey will take them to fill out: the message 'This will take around x minutes to complete' should appear on the first screen online and the first page on paper. If you feel uncomfortable about putting in the correct length of time because it is off-putting, reduce the survey!

Acting on the outcomes of surveys is of course essential, and if it's possible to acknowledge the respondents and tell them how their views have impacted the library, that in itself is great marketing. Cambridge University's Andy Priestner (a case study contributor in Chapter 9) has learnt that the personal approach is worth the time it takes:

> I only have to look at the huge range of comments on our annual survey to realize how different each and every student is in terms of their outlook, skills and needs. This is why I took it upon myself to reply to each and every comment personally – hugely time-consuming but judging from the subsequent gratitude and new understandings that were reached, incalculably valuable too. Where possible we need to create opportunities for personal 1-to-1 interactions through all the mediums and avenues open to us.

Focus groups

Focus groups are a chance to really get detailed information. When run well they can yield huge amounts of useful data, so it's worth providing incentives for respondents. Many advocate giving them all a $5 Starbucks card (or similar) and inviting participants to spend it on coffee and cakes to bring to the focus group meeting itself. For ten respondents that would mean an outlay of $50, but as Rebecca Jones puts it: ' . . . yes, invest $50 to save $500 on continuing the wrong service!'

Rebecca is a partner with Dysart & Jones Associates (www.dysartjones.com); she works with organizations, including libraries in public, corporate and academic environments. In this next case study she gives an expert view on how to organize a really effective focus group.

Case study 2: Gaining feedback from library users and non-users | Rebecca Jones

Early in my career a senior manager encouraged me to view feedback as a gift. The individual or group is *feeding* their opinions and reactions to our services or our actions *back* to us, allowing us to see our libraries through their lenses in their contexts. We may not always like the gifts or the feedback we receive, and we are free to do what we wish with gifts or feedback – either use it or reject it.

One way to gather feedback from library users and non-users is to conduct group interviews or focus groups. For the purpose of this case study the terms are used synonymously. This technique, conducted properly, can provide the library with incredible insights to consider and act on.

So, how does a library properly conduct a focus group? First, by clarifying the purpose. This seems obvious, but too often it is at this initial step that focus groups start to go off track. The library must be very clear on *what* it wants to know to then determine *who* needs to be involved in the group and *how* the group must be conducted.

What is it that the library wants to know? Focus groups are a technique for gathering qualitative input regarding a service offering (from a specific program to opening hours to facilities, etc.), future plans or, really, any library data, concept, activity or issue. What does the library want to know at the end of the focus group that it doesn't know now? Does the library have quantitative data from a survey that it needs to better understand? Is the library developing its strategic plan, and wants to understand how its services and facilities are perceived by the community or, in the academic environment, by students or faculty?

Specific example: a public library developing a five-year strategic plan had conducted a web survey to inform its strategies for future services. Based on the data collected and the environmental scan, they drafted three scenarios for potential services. They determined the purpose of focus groups was to:

- test these scenarios and gain the participants' honest reactions
- gather ideas and insights for refining or altering these scenarios, and for developing effective marketing programs for the services.

Who needs to participate in the focus group? The purpose of the group defines the characteristics of the ideal participants. In the example cited above, the participants needed to represent the various groups in the community served by the library. This included a range of ages, occupations and preferences or behaviours, which meant users and non-users. Libraries are usually quite good at recruiting users as participants for focus groups, but find it much more challenging to recruit non-users. This doesn't need to be the case. Every library employee has family members or friends who aren't library users; in fact, every user knows people who don't use the library. Recruiting people, both users and non-users, requires a clear, compelling invitation and, quite honestly, food – either at the focus group or after, perhaps in the form of a gift certificate. Invite users to attend and to bring a friend who doesn't use the library; be clear in the invitation that there will be food and refreshments for all those attending and, for those who bring a friend who is not a library user, an additional $5.00 gift certificate for a popular coffee shop for both the user and their friend. We've conducted focus groups in busy corporations using this approach, and the focus groups have been full.

Another specific example: we recently conducted group interviews for a public library of youth in a community to:

- identify the types of services of interest to them, and
- phrases that may be meaningful to youth in marketing the services.

Notice that the purpose of the group interviews was not to identify specific services, but rather 'types of services of interest.' It's important to keep in mind that group interviews aren't prescriptive or absolute; they are a mechanism for gathering reactions and perspectives, which may change.

The library easily identified teenagers who regularly use the library to invite, but was dubious about getting teens that were non-users to participate. We asked each of these 'patron' teens to bring a friend who doesn't use the library. Their compensation would be pizza, soft drinks, plus two hours community service credits. The result? The group interviews were well attended with equal numbers of patron/non-patron teens.

Focus groups should have 13–16 participants. This number of people allows meaningful, effective discussion of the questions. Since a focus group should not be longer than 90 minutes, any more than 16 people limits the amount of participation for each individual. If the focus group is discussing ten questions, that's nine minutes per question with each individual having less than one minute to contribute their input.

Many focus group organizers prefer to form each group with individuals sharing common characteristics (e.g. in public libraries: a group for youth; another for adults aged 25–55; another for adults aged 55+; another for parents of pre-schoolers, etc. In corporations, a group for users, and another for non-users, etc. In academic libraries, a group for faculty from a specific department, etc.). While this approach is valid, it can also be extremely effective to mix groups. Often the participants find the discussion interesting as they hear different, possibly divergent, views.

How should the group be conducted? The decision to use an external facilitator depends on whether the library has people on staff capable of conducting the group and maintaining subjectivity. It's critical that the facilitator is capable of managing the discussion, ensuring an equitable, safe exchange of views among the participants. Although an emotional or disrespectful exchange is rare, the facilitator needs to be skilled in mitigating and managing this when it does occur. The session should begin with the facilitator welcoming the group and clarifying the session's purpose, timing, ground rules and how this information will be used.

Ideally the questions or topics to be discussed are sent to the participants prior to the focus group. Not only does this allow people to think about their responses prior to the group, but conveys to participants that this is a quality process and that their time and contribution is greatly appreciated.

The group doesn't need to be conducted in a room with two-way mirrors, although if such a facility is available and affordable, then it is an excellent option and allows library management to hear the focus group. At a minimum the group needs to be led by a facilitator with someone documenting the group discussion and recording it. The focus group findings are then based on the facilitator and the documenter's notes and observations as well as the recording.

The facilitator and documenter should produce a report of the findings and discuss this, in detail, with the library. A report should also be prepared and distributed to focus group participants. People who have participated in a well run focus group are usually very interested in the information collected in the group(s) and how this information will be used. The report shouldn't be as detailed as the report prepared for the library but should convey the key points gathered from the groups. This report to the participants is, in addition to the incentive or refreshments provided at the time of the group, a thank you to the participants for the gift they've given to the library.

Asking people

A final (and hugely undervalued) way to get feedback is simply to ask people. I asked Justin Hoenke (who provides a case study in Chapter 7, 'Marketing with New Technologies') which single tool he'd recommend to help market a library. He replied: 'It's a pretty simple tool that every library can afford. Talk to your patrons. Ask them what they want in their library. You'll be surprised at how many great ideas they have. Once they know you're serious about listening to their requests, that's when you know you've created an engaged library user.'

This approach is so unscientific that most libraries would dismiss it as a legitimate technique, but it can be really useful as part of a wider strategy. When a user comes to the enquiry desk and you've dealt with their query, why not ask them an important question? Such as: 'What do you think of the new refurbishment?', 'Can you find the materials you need easily?', 'What's the one area you'd like us to focus investment in over the next few years – is it the space, or the collections, or the facilities?' Or, 'Do you use social media and if so on which platforms would you like to interact with the library?' Gathering answers to questions of this kind can give you a real feel for what your users think, and help inform decision-making along with the cold hard data recorded via surveys and focus groups.

Another important mechanism for feedback is social monitoring – that is, listening to what your users say about your library and related issues on social media sites. We'll look at that in more detail later on, in Chapter 6, 'Marketing with Social Media'.

Prioritizing feedback

Constraints of both time and money mean libraries won't always be able to act on good suggestions they get from user feedback. If prioritization is required, a simple but effective way of doing this is to rate each suggestion out of ten for both 'ease of implementation' (with ten being the easiest, one being the hardest) and 'impact' if they were implemented (ten constituting the biggest possible impact, and one the smallest).

Plotting the results on a simple quadrant quickly shows which ideas should be prioritized – those closest to the top right-hand corner are the best combination of easy to implement and high-impact.

Figure 2.2 on the next page is an example with four ideas. Idea 1 is high impact but difficult to achieve, and Idea 2 is easy to do but with relatively small gains; both may be worth pursuing depending on resources. Idea 4 certainly isn't worth bothering with, but Idea 3 is the clear winner, combining great impact with relative ease of implementation:

If your goal is to increase use of resources by existing users, user feedback should form the basis of your analysis and your plans. However, if the goal is

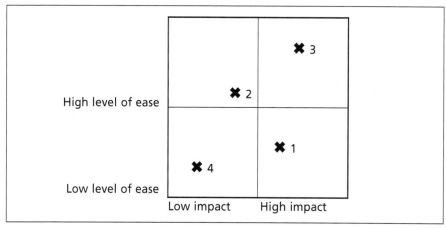

Figure 2.2 *Prioritizing feedback*

to increase the number of users using the library in total, an understanding of non-users is absolutely essential to give you the kind of knowledge to help enable such a shift. At this stage your analysis should be about what the library already offers non-users which they don't know about (but would use if they did), and what the library could *potentially* offer non-users to meet their needs in the future.

Finally, a really useful avenue of feedback comes from lapsed users. People who previously had the time and inclination to visit the library but no longer do so can offer absolutely vital insight into what wasn't working for them, which in turn can lead to better user retention in the future.

Any number of textbooks detail how to go about performing a SWOT analysis on your library – to identify the Strengths, Weaknesses, Opportunities and Threats – so I won't go into that here. One thing to stress, though, is that when considering your institution's assets it is worth looking beyond just its books and other information resources. It could be the library space or the location, which would mean you should market the library as destination. It could be the courses and community groups you run. It could be that your staff are your main asset, in which case don't be afraid to market *them*.

It's likely that each of these will be assets for different groups of users or potential users – this is where segmentation becomes so important.

3 Segmentation

You've decided on where you want to be, and you've analysed your own library, your competitors, and your respective positions within the market. The next stage is segmentation, the formal term for one of the seven key concepts discussed in Chapter 1: creating different offers for different groups of users and would-be users. The process is twofold: it involves first deciding how best to divide up the groups of people to whom you are marketing and secondly developing different value propositions for each of them. In essence this means showing each of the many 'faces' of the library to each different group as appropriate, marketing the aspect of your service provision that most appeals to them. It is an instructive process, allowing you to really explore what you have and how it can be beneficial to different groups, and sometimes it exposes holes in the library provision. Sometimes you find out that you don't really have anything to offer a particular group, but that group falls within the library's remit and so needs to be accommodated: in that instance, you may need to create some kind of new service that forms the basis of a brand-new value proposition.

Perhaps the trickiest part is choosing how to segment your different target groups. I would recommend a hierarchy that begins with two major groups, users and non-users, and then sub-divides each of these into smaller segments; beyond that, every library will be different and segmentation is not an exact science. It could be that many groups appear in both categories – for example, in the academic environment you could have 'taught postgraduates' as a segment. Taught postgraduates may represent a major hole in your usage stats: it could be that the vast majority of them ignore the library entirely, meaning they're a big target for your marketing to non-users. However, those that currently *do* use the library still need a certain amount of attention, particularly if any of them can be cultivated into library champions to spread the word to their peers – and if your marketing works successfully and many more taught postgraduates start using the library, they will need to be marketed to in order to retain them.

To continue the academic library example in order to contextualize segmentation in the real world, other segments might include research students, academic staff, undergraduates, distance learners, lifelong learners, emeritus staff (all of whom could be further sub-divided into arts and humanities, sciences and social sciences if the market research shows these groups behave differently in their use of the library) and support staff.

At the end of the process of segmentation, the aim should be to have several distinct groups to which you'll market the library. You should know roughly how big each group is and how important each group is – this helps prioritize your promotional efforts. You should know what each group's needs are, and whether or not they are currently being met by the library. This should lead to the formation of an offer – a different value proposition, focusing on the most appropriate strengths in the library service – for each segment or group.

Segmenting your existing users

Not all library users are the same, obviously, and it is tempting to divide them into obvious demographics: young and old, male and female, local and remote, and so on. But it may be more useful to divide them up by their information-seeking behaviour, their motivations, because that crosses traditional boundaries of age and gender and location, and ultimately determines what kind of offer they would like to receive from the library. How you segment your market ties in closely with what your aims are – if, for example, one of your aims is to get existing users to use your resources in greater volume, then dividing them up into 'casual users' and 'power users' could be beneficial, as it will allow you to concentrate your marketing efforts into the former segment to try and make them more like the latter. In practice this might mean outreach to the casual users via e-mail or postal mail-shots promoting the more advanced services which power users commonly enjoy, or starting a campaign on social media to get your followers to visit the building in person more often. Preaching to the converted (the power users) has its uses in marketing, but when resources are limited segmentation provides a great way of ensuring they're used in the areas where the most potential gains are to be had.

Segmenting your non-users

If one of your aims is to increase the number of users your library has, then segmenting your non-users into different target demographics is terrifically useful. Once you break down the potential audience for your marketing, everything seems infinitely more achievable: rather than trying to achieve a blanket aim like 'get 500 extra members' you can start thinking like a marketer, and set specific objectives (more on which below) such as 'I want 100 more users from the 65+ market, 200 more parents and their kids, 50 more remote users and at least 50 casual users who mainly come for the free Wi-Fi but eventually start using other resources too'. When you have targets like these, the whole process of marketing becomes much more focused and specific: you create offers designed to appeal to each segment, and then you market to them and record the numbers and evaluate the campaigns.

Targeting the currently indifferent

The temptation will be to base most of your marketing around the 'existing users' segment – it's comforting and comfortable to market to those who already class themselves as avid library fans. I would argue that we have to be braver and put more of our resources into the non-user segment, most particularly in the public library sector. We have to target those people running from A to B, head-down, and show them we can help them on their journey.

At the moment, at both industry level and sometimes at the level of individual libraries, we put much of our resources into retaining existing users or trying to convert people who are actively hostile to libraries. In fact, the former don't need as much persuasion to keep using the library, and the latter are probably a lost cause not worth pursuing. It's the *currently indifferent* at whom we should be targeting much of our marketing – those who would find value in the services we offer if they (a) knew the services existed and (b) had the benefits clearly explained to them in language they understand. To use an election analogy, we currently spend too much money on the people who've already made up their minds who they're voting for. It's the floating voters and, perhaps even more importantly, the people who don't even realize there's an election taking place, who represent the best return on our marketing investment.

All of the processes described above allow you to set objectives (for example, to meet currently unmet needs in the future) and, later, to determine which messages you wish to market to each group via your promotional activities.

4 Set objectives

Objectives are distinct from goals or aims because, while the latter describe the overall ambition, objectives describe the specific methods of achieving it. We've asked where we want to be; now we must ask how we get there. Only at this stage, when you've researched the market, understood where you stand within that market and segmented it into different groups, can you now set the objectives for exactly what you want your marketing to achieve in each area.

As mentioned above, putting numbers on your objectives is a great way to focus the mind. It helps you understand not just what needs to be done, but *how* it can be done. You may not hit all your targets, of course (new members, people through the turnstiles, circulation, website use or whatever they may be) but this in itself is instructive and can be used to inform future campaigns.

Objectives should be as specific as possible, as measurable as possible, and preferably dated too. Of all sections of the marketing cycle, this one and the next are what constitute the action plan your library will follow.

5 Promotional activities

Finally we get to the actual promotion itself. This book is essentially full of information about promotional activities, so I won't go into detail here, but in short it is at this stage that you start to *implement* your marketing campaigns, be they online, on paper or in person. All the work you've done on market research and segmentation by this stage should mean you know exactly who you are marketing to, and what you want to say to each group.

If there is one overarching rule here, it is to decide on clear messages. Many of the problems libraries have in marketing themselves stem from the fact that many people don't really understand what we do. We have to communicate our value to each segment as simply as possible. And remember, marketing is a conversation – your promotional activities should allow for two-way interaction.

6 Measurement

I can't stress enough how vital measurement is – measurement is *what makes this marketing*. If you don't measure the impact of what you've done, you can't really complete the cycle by evaluating and then improving your offer. Ideally you should be able to measure the number of people who've been impacted by each marketing campaign you run, and the number of times the campaign has had an impact. So, for a website that would be the number of unique visitors and the number of page views; for a poster, the number of people who see it and the number of times it is seen. From this it should be possible to calculate how much it cost to reach each person in a particular way, and from there you can calculate which marketing methods, approaches and campaigns represent the best use of your resources.

As part of a strategic marketing plan, you should aim to measure not just the marketing campaigns themselves but the changes in user behaviour that come about as a result.

For this stage of the cycle we have an expert view from Alison Circle.

Case study 3: Measurement in marketing Columbus Metropolitan Library | Alison Circle

Alison Circle is Director of Marketing and Strategic Planning for Columbus Metropolitan Library. She has more than 20 years' experience in marketing, including corporate and not-for-profit companies. She writes a marketing column for Library Journal and speaks extensively on the subject. In this expert view she picks up on many of the key themes in this chapter (including a working example of Segmentation), and explains the need to measure outcomes rather than outputs.

Columbus Metropolitan Library (CML) is recognized as one of the best libraries in the United States. An important driver to our success has been an early adoption of marketing practice. In an industry that promises 'Open to All,' in today's fractured marketplace we can't be all things to all people. So how did we begin? We started with research – a deep examination into the *behaviour* of our customers – segmenting our customer data into behavioural clusters: Young Minds (children); Power Users (avid readers and the mainstay of public library use); Virtual Users (computer users). We have 15 clusters overall; we chose 3 for our primary focus and drove all of our efforts toward these strategies. We were committed to doing a few things very well.

Next we rebranded the institution. Previously, staff who wanted to start a program or service got a logo, but CML had grown too many brands and lacked structure or coherence. Our logo itself was stuck in a box. Literally. It was a blue square box in need of updating. Using our strategic plan to drive key programs, we created a brand architecture system to organize our services into a family of products.

It was vitally important to bring library staff along through this change process. Staff were used to – and enjoyed – creating their own promotional pieces. As the organization centralized the marketing function and message development, it became critical for all promotion – large and small – to be co-ordinated centrally.

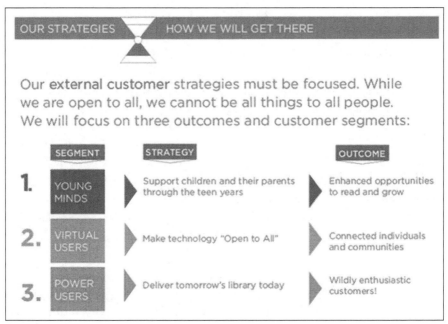

Figure 2.3 *CML's external customers strategies*

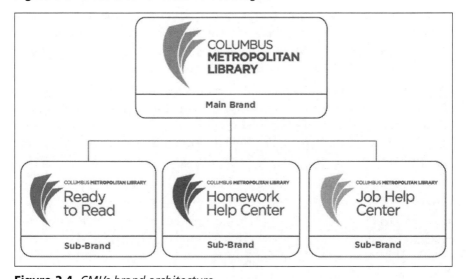

Figure 2.4 *CML's brand architecture*

To help accomplish this, CML turned to a book (naturally!): *Managing Transitions* by William Bridges (2009). This book gave CML the language and tools to recognize and address the process of change. For some staff, making posters was the fun part of their job, and we were taking that away. That loss needed to be

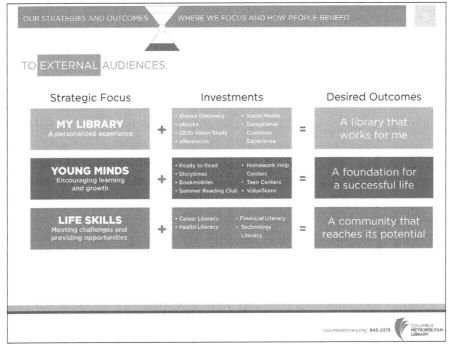

Figure 2.5 *CML's strategies and outcomes*

recognized and addressed. I'm happy to say that we have made tremendous progress and (mostly) speak with a single voice. In a world crowded with noise, this has become more important than ever.

One of my favourite behaviour quotes is from Jack Welch, business icon, who said: 'If you can't measure it, it's a hobby.' And that means going beyond counting (outputs), to measuring behavioural change (outcomes). It isn't enough to know how many kids signed into the Homework Help Center. In today's marketplace we need to show the value of the Homework Help Center: did kids' grades improve? Are we driving up graduation rates? Gathering this information is hard work. But 'gut instinct' or 'feelings' can no longer drive business decisions.

I'm thrilled to say the payoff of our approach has been great. With this framework, we are able to tell the library's story; it led to our designation as National Library of the Year.

What's next? We've updated our strategic plan to drive deeper change and deliver on our lofty vision of 'a thriving community where wisdom prevails.' And while you won't see our customer clusters in this new plan, the thinking behind customer segmentation continues to be the backbone of our strategy.

7 Evaluation

Once you've measured your marketing efforts, you can evaluate what worked and what didn't – this relates directly back to your goals from the very first stage, and your objectives later on. The process enables you to market better the next time around: either doing more with the same resources, or potentially being able to achieve the same with less. For those of us trying to embed marketing into the wider culture of our institutions, evaluation also serves the essential role of providing evidence of the return on our investment (or ROI) in the promotional process. In order to continue to be allowed to spend funds on marketing, we must prove we are spending them wisely.

To evaluate a marketing effort, it is not sufficient just to look at the numbers. You must ask the question: did people do what we tried to persuade them to do with our marketing? So, for example, perhaps you pushed your Facebook site over the summer, and got 500 extra likes/followers. The figure of 500 is the measurement, so what is the evaluation? If the aim was simply to get more followers then of course you have been successful, but if your aim was to affect behavioural change, with liking the Facebook page the first step on a process which ends with a new user signing up for a library card, then you must evaluate whether your 500 likes achieved this or not.

Every marketing effort should feed into the next, when properly evaluated. Mistakes won't be repeated, strengths will be built upon, new techniques and technologies will be accurately assessed for their usefulness.

8 Modification

It is absolutely crucial not to leave out this last stage! You've planned and run and evaluated your marketing, you know what worked and what didn't, and you can see where things can be changed and improved. So act on it, and modify your approach so it works better next time around.

Remember, the changes you implement shouldn't only be based on your experiences last time around, but should take into account the changing environments and cultural landscape in which your library sits.

Developing a marketing plan

So what does all this mean in practice, in the real world of day-to-day library life? Ultimately all of this should be fodder for a strategic marketing plan: a document which tells the library how to proceed. Preferably in as brief and straightforward a way as possible, so that the plan doesn't inhibit action. Considering all of the above, a strategic marketing plan might be based around a structure like this:

1 **Executive Summary** An overview of the entire marketing plan.
2 **Goals** Where you want the library to be within the time-frame of this marketing plan; what you want the marketing efforts to achieve; how these relate to the overall strategic plan of the library.
3 **Internal campaign details** Marketing works best as a collective effort across the library – this section should detail how the goals, objectives and promotional methods will be conveyed internally.
4 **Market research** A breakdown of the community of users and potential users; analysis of your competition including competitive benchmarking; analysis of your own library services, including user feedback.
5 **Segmentation of the market** The division of your market into groups based on behaviour, motivation and needs; analysis of how the library currently meets each group's needs; prioritization of each group; and the proposed offer for each group.
6 **Objectives** Specific methods for achieving the marketing goals, preferably involving targets for growth based on increases by segment. This is really the action plan.
7 **Promotion: methods and activities** The nuts and bolts of your marketing campaign – the key messages, and the platforms by which they'll be delivered.
8 **Methods of measurement** Details of how the success or failure of the marketing will be measured and recorded.
9 **Framework for evaluation** How and when the campaign will be evaluated; information from previous campaigns' evaluation if applicable.
10 **Areas of responsibility** Which departments and/or individuals will be responsible for implementing which areas of the plan.
11 **Cost analysis** How much the marketing campaign will cost, in terms of both financial outlay and staff time.
12 **Modification** The final section to be completed at the end of the campaign – how will any of the processes above be improved or changed next time around?

More information, links, and further reading including sample marketing plans, are available online at **www.librarymarketingtoolkit.com/p/strategic-marketing.html**.

other institutions in which people may wish to invest their time rather than investing it in libraries.

The brand, on the other hand, is the sum total of everyone's perceptions about what you do. It is the way people feel about your library, the way people describe your library to others. Clearly, branding as a marketing practice is an attempt to influence this as favourably as possible. But the brand is in the eye of the beholder – in the eyes of the users and the non-users of your library – so you can never fully control it. It encompasses your visual identity, your building, your books, your e-resources, your triumphs, your mistakes, your history, your position in the community, your staff, your *reputation*. To put it a simpler way, a brand exists in the way people feel about something; branding is the attempt to make those feelings positive. Your library is already emitting signals about itself to anyone who is interested, so you may as well try and influence those signals.

Visual identity is the sum total of the way everything looks and the messages this puts out – the building, the layout, the books, the leaflets, the guides, the presentation materials; all of it. It is aesthetics, ergonomics, and semiotics too.

What is library branding?

The use of terminology like 'branding' in association with libraries fills many information professionals with horror. It is the kind of management-speak that seems at odds with the very fundamentals of offering a free, neutral public service to those who need it. But all branding really means is offering a consistent and identifiable library service which is recognizably yours. This chapter focuses somewhat on visual identity, but it is important to establish that visual identity is a part of branding, rather than the other way around. The library brand encompasses far more than the aesthetics – the way front-line staff interact with users is part of the brand. The decision to have a member of staff stand in the foyer to greet and smile at the users is part of a branding exercise, but equally the decision *not* to do this also feeds into the library brand.

We all know that a good impression is much easier to undo than a bad one; people only need to have one negative experience of an institution for that to dominate their entire perception of it. In sport there is a cliché which footballers in particular like to trot out with great regularity: you are only as good as your last game. What they mean is that their reputation is influenced

CHAPTER 3
The library brand

Branding is a big issue. Marketing serves many functions, not least to boost reputation; with that in mind, it shouldn't stop once your users are through the door.

There are many elements to a library brand, and several are covered in the following pages (another key aspect, the library building itself, gets its own thorough investigation in Chapter 4), starting with creating or updating the library's visual identity. This includes a case study from Jessica Wykes of City University, who takes us through design on a shoestring. A library brand can be boosted by some well considered merchandise, and the successful 'Sshhh...!' bags merchandizing campaign at the University of Leeds, run by Katy Sidwell, is the subject of the second case study. Finally there is the tricky issue of branding the library in conjunction with another, related, organization: Stephen Pinfield talks us through marketing a converged library and IT service at Nottingham University in the third case study.

Quick definitions

Before we go any further, we should define the key terms for this chapter Firstly, there is an important distinction to establish, between the term 'branding' and 'brand'.

Branding is the process of creating a recognizable product or service building an identity which people understand – and marketing it as disti from potential competitors. In the case of libraries the competition is necessarily within the industry; while you may want to compete with ot libraries in the area, there is a much bigger battle going on which pit libraries against bookshops, against the internet and against all mann hugely by the most recent thing they've done (even though by rights it should be the sum of all their achievements and failings) – so if someone reaches the final of a tournament and then chokes (in other words, doesn't perform due to the pressure and ultimately loses) they will be known as a 'choker' rather than as a 'silver medallist'.

To an extent this is analogous to librarianship. The reputation of each library is only as good as its last customer interaction. This is of course a huge over-simplification, but the fact is that if you serve every customer superbly there will gradually be a net gain in the reputation of your institution; serve one rudely or lazily and there may well be an instant reputation plummet. Word of mouth is so important, and research has shown that the majority of people are more likely to pass on bad experiences than good ones.

Reputation is the general esteem in which something or someone is held. This general esteem is easy to perceive as a fixed constant, a largely solid and static 'thing' which is sometimes influenced by particularly significant events. The reality for something like a library is that reputation is a constantly updating, evolving and shifting entity, held in the collective (and individual) consciousness of both the library's users and even people who've never set foot on its premises.

Elizabeth Esteve-Coll (1985) put it this way, back in the 1980s: 'The library is not an abstraction. It has an identity, an identity created by the staff contact with the users.' That remains true today. So while this isn't a book about staff management and I wouldn't presume to tell you how to ensure your staff are friendly, it's worth remembering that everything else in this volume will count for nought if, when the target audience finally make it onto your premises, they are treated rudely.

Ultimately, the aim of an organization's branding and visual identity is not just to give a good impression, but to help people position that organization within their lifestyle. It helps people make a decision as to whether something is 'for them' or not. You need to understand your demographics and potential demographics, and then brand your library to appeal to them. In the modern economic climate, it is no longer sufficient just to provide a service for those who know about it; libraries need to package themselves up in such a way as to draw new audiences in. Branding doesn't just increase use of the library by attracting new customers; it also increases the amount of use by existing customers, and influences those decision makers who hold the purse-strings for library finance.

Visual identity

The benefits of a strong visual identity are many. It makes your brand more easily memorable. It makes you stand out. It allows you to say more with less; you don't have to use up lots of space on a poster or website explaining who you are, if your visual identity is quickly recognizable. And it unites and gives cohesion to multiple aspects of the library – or even multiple libraries within the same authority, site or organization.

Six steps to create or improve your house style

A cohesive house style is a key part of branding and visual identity. Preferably it should set your library apart from others, but at the very least it needs to be functional, attractive and accessible. As with all aspects of marketing, there are no hard and fast rules for what is the 'right' house style – it depends on your demographic, and on the personality of your organization.

Creating a strong house style doesn't need to take an enormous amount of time or investment, and it can yield instant and lasting rewards. Whether you are working to improve one that is already in place, or are creating one from scratch, these six steps are all important. (Working within the limits of a house style imposed on you from above is covered in Chapter 9.)

1 Do your homework

The visual identity and house style must suit your library and your demographic. It isn't automatically better to create something incredibly hip and modern – this wouldn't necessarily work for an 18th-century archive, for example. A five-floor city library has a completely different brand to a small-town library with just two rooms. If possible a visual identity should play to your existing strengths and existing customers' expectations, but try and move the brand into territory that appeals to potential new demographics as well. It's a mixture of how you are seen, and how you want to be seen.

It is easy enough to find out how people currently perceive the library – ask them. You can create a simple, short survey aimed at existing users, which you leave next to the self-issue machines or on the reference desk, then recreate it online and promote it via social media. It could consist of questions such as:

1 Which three words do you most associate with the library?
2 What are the library's main strengths? And our three main weaknesses?
3 What are your favourite brands outside of libraries? (Make a list of options for the respondent to tick, including modern brands like Apple, and more traditional brands too.)
4 Which of these features would you like to see the library introduce? (Again, make a list for them to choose from, made up of traditional library services and very modern, edgier things.)
5 If you're happy to hear more about what the library has planned in the coming months, please leave your name and e-mail address.

Then create a similar survey aimed at those who don't currently use the library (replace question 2 with 'What stops you from using the library?' and change question 4 to 'Which of these features would make you more likely to give the library a try?'), and get out onto the streets and get some feedback from non-users – spend an afternoon gathering views. If this is for a public library ask to leave paper copies of the survey in local grocery stores or bookshops; in an academic library ask to leave paper copies in academic departments. Promote the non-user survey on Twitter and ask people to retweet a link to it; research has shown that simply asking people to RT makes a huge difference as to how often a tweet is retweeted (as long as you don't ask people to do this too often). A Tweet retweeted will reach a whole new audience of people who don't currently use the library.

The results of the questionnaire will tell you what existing and potential customers think of the library brand as it stands, what other kinds of brand they associate with their lifestyle, and what direction they'd like to see the library go in. Crucially, you may also get the names of users and would-be users to whom you can promote the library via e-mail, and potentially ask them for more feedback in the future.

The final factor in gaining feedback this way is to incentivize the questionnaire, and make this incentive relevant. If it's possible to offer a prize draw that relates to your library, that's a great opportunity. For example, if you run classes for which you charge, the prize could be a voucher for one session's worth of training; or if you have a library shop, the prize could be a gift certificate for that. For the questionnaire aimed at those who aren't existing library users, an Amazon voucher is always welcome, as you can buy so many different things with it – but you can still promote it in library terms, for example: 'Complete the questionnaire to be entered into a prize draw for

£50's worth of Amazon vouchers. And of course, you can always visit the library and borrow all the books and music you want for free . . .'

The other aspect of doing your homework involves deciding which elements of your output are going to be branded with your house style. Library materials or elements to which house style or visual identity might be applied may include all or some of the following:

- leaflets, guides, work-books and brochures
- letter-heads, envelopes and business cards
- posters and notices
- signs
- shelving
- web pages
- social media profiles
- online and paper newsletters
- presentations (e.g. PowerPoint slides)
- advertising
- merchandise and give-aways such as library-branded pens, bookmarks, etc.
- staff uniforms, if you have them.

2 Make it accessible

For most public-sector institutions, making your services and materials accessible to those with a disability is a legal requirement. Even where this isn't the case, it is ethically sound to avoid excluding sections of society from being able to function comfortably within the library and when using the library's printed and web output.

This has a significant impact on the visual identity of your library because you can't simply choose the colours, fonts and designs you want with entirely free rein; certain standards must be adhered to in order to ensure everyone can make use of your materials. When out-sourcing a visual identity or any element of design (such as a logo) it is important to remember the onus is on you as a library to provide accurate guidelines that result in an accessible product. The provider or designer will probably not do this automatically.

There is plenty of detailed information available online about accessibility standards (links provided below) but there are a few basic rules it is good to remember at all times, whether you are out-sourcing or designing in-house:

Colour

1 Colour perception varies enormously between individuals. Contrary to popular belief, there is no one colour scheme which is definitively accessible, or inaccessible, to everyone (although red and green used together is always a bad idea, as these are the two most commonly indistinguishable colours for those who struggle with colour recognition). It's more important to ensure high contrast between the words and what they're written on – two different shades of blue would be an obvious no-no, as would pastel type on a white background, and so on. Light against dark, or dark against light, is best.

2 On a related note, text over a patterned background or over a detailed photograph, reduces the contrast and so makes it harder to read. This applies not just to people who are colour-blind, partially sighted or dyslexic, but to assistive software such as screen-readers, too.

3 Make sure colour isn't central to the user's ability to use the materials. For example a printed leaflet which says 'all recommendations are in orange' or a web application which says 'press the red button to continue' would be problematic, as would graphs or charts which rely solely on colour to differentiate between fields.

Web materials specifically

1 Images should be described using the <title> text tag, as should any graphs or other graphics, animations and other multimedia. The <alt> tag should provide an alternative if the image doesn't load for any reason.

2 Audio sections should have the option of a written transcript available.

3 Hyperlinks should be sentences or chunks of sentences to give them context, rather than a single word. Let's take a link to a library's foreign literature pages as an example. It is never acceptable to write: 'to view the library's foreign literature pages, click here.' Much better to hyperlink an entire sentence, such as 'You can view the library's foreign literature pages here.' When hovered over, links should give clear instructions as to what will happen when they're clicked (via the <title> tag), for example 'Go to the library's foreign literature pages.'

Printed materials specifically

1 Alternative formats such as audio or Braille should at the very least be

provided on request, and information about this should be clearly available.

2 Legibility is impaired by any kind of reflection or glare – for this reason, glossier brochures can be problematic. Quality matt looks fine and avoids those issues.

3 Font size: 12pt should be the minimum.

4 Consistency is important in terms of layout – page numbers in the same place on each page, for example.

Fonts for all media

There is much debate as to whether serif or sans-serif fonts are best from an accessibility point of view – as there is no conclusive proof either way, both can be used in printed publications. However as a general rule, 'cursive' fonts (those that try and resemble writing or brush-strokes) are best avoided entirely.

It is worth noting that large blocks of *italic text*, **bold text**, underlined text or CAPITAL LETTERS are best avoided too. They're fine in moderation, although generally speaking **bold** is more friendly than *italics* from an accessibility point of view.

Using fresh and non-standard fonts makes a surprisingly huge difference to how good a poster or presentation looks: download some from FontSquirrel (at www.fontsquirrel.com) for free. At my own institution we use 'Leitura Sans Grot', a non-standard font not usually featured in the Microsoft Office suite, in all our branding and visual identity across the library and IT services.

More info

The above is really just a précis of the main principles of accessibility. For large projects it is worth checking out the official literature for more detailed information – it's all available online, and the following are places I'd recommend for further reading:

- Royal National Institute of Blind People (RNIB) guidelines:
  www.rnib.org.uk/professionals/accessibleinformation/Pages/
  accessible_information.aspx
- Web Accessibility Initiative (W3C):
  www.w3.org/WAI/intro/accessibility.php

- Web Accessibility in Mind (WebAIM):
  http://webaim.org/

3 Choose a colour palette

The easiest way to create a distinct visual identity is through colour. Something as simple as having a purple logo and purple text on a cream background is a colour palette that can be applied across numerous disparate media and still maintain a cohesive feel, even if the designs have little else in common.

Use a consistent colour scheme and style that will work across all media. This is fairly obvious stuff but people still sometimes forget exactly where their visual identity will end up. For example, if you choose light colours that work well against a black background that'll work fine online, but won't work so well when you come to brand your printed materials. It's a good idea to have two opposite versions of the same colour scheme – in other words, to have a 'reversible' visual identity. For example, if your regular colour palette is to use red ink on a white background, this won't work so well among darker coloured materials – in which case you can use white ink on a red background instead, and maintain the visual identity.

4 Invest in design

By invest in design, I don't necessarily mean investing money in outsourcing to a designer – although certainly that can pay dividends. Primarily I mean invest yourself in the process of creating a powerful design that reflects your library – put the time and resources into doing it well. Some practical points:

1 Very modern and edgy designs will look great initially but may date more quickly. In my view, contemporary without being too inclined towards a particular design fad is better.
2 You can get more applications out of a logo if it is a combination of a symbol and a 'wordmark' – a wordmark is the name of the institution written in a distinct (and often unique) way. A logo containing both of these can be used as is, and also split up into its constituent parts where space is an issue.
3 Vector graphics use plotted points instead of pixels – if you can create and store your logos, symbols, wordmarks and so on using vector artwork, it can be blown up or reduced to any size without losing fidelity

(unlike pixel-based graphics which, as the name implies, become pixellated and blurry when up-scaled too far).

4 When choosing a font for your web applications, remember that not all browsers have all fonts available, and will only be able to show the closest equivalent if they don't have a particular font installed.

Academic libraries, in particular, shouldn't overlook the mutual benefits of asking suitable students for assistance. Final-year or Masters-level photographers, designers, copywriters, analysts and even marketers could provide really useful and imaginative input to a marketing campaign's promotional materials. They get valuable experience at minimal cost to the library (though we should be careful not to over-use them), and represent an excellent alternative to one member of library staff attempting to be the jack of all trades.

Much of marketing is digital now, yet good old-fashioned printed materials still play a pivotal role in promoting the library. Outsourcing these can certainly be costly, but poorly produced materials in-house can cause reputational harm. Good quality materials can be made within the library, however. At City University in London, Jessica Wykes is Subject Librarian for Assistive Technologies and Marketing – she offers expert advice on achieving great design with minimal outlay.

Case study 4: Designing on a shoestring | Jessica Wykes

Background

At City University Library we mostly create promotional materials for resources and services in-house, on a limited budget, rather than outsource. With an interest in graphic design, I found myself taking on more and more design work until it became a formal part of my role. Even though qualified graphic designers may see this as sacrilege, I feel that you can teach yourself some of the basics and that it is possible to create some effective work when these new skills are combined with first-hand knowledge of your institution, its values and its customers.

Approach

When beginning work on a project, sketch it out (with old-fashioned pen and paper) so that you can see harmony between the main elements which can help you to visualize the overall shape. Spend a bit of time thinking about what you expect from the final project taking into account, size, shape, budget and shelf-life of the finished product. All of these factors will have a bearing on the design – for example, is it a good idea to include web addresses and very particular staff details if you are designing an exhibition banner to use at a range of events for a long time to come? If there is no budget for printing you could design your work for online viewing in free online services like Issuu (at http://issuu.com).

Sourcing and working with images

Although what can be achieved simply with font and colour shouldn't be underestimated, images play a key part in our marketing materials. There are many ways you can get hold of good images. You could buy one or more great stock images; for example iStockphoto (www.istockphoto.com) have thousands of really great professional images. Microsoft images and Flickr also have some really good ones and some for free, but make sure you check the copyright and usage permissions.

However, sometimes stock images can be a little clichéd or impersonal, so try taking your own pictures. There is something unique about this that can help library users connect and be excited by what you are promoting. We photograph library users (or sometimes temporary members of staff) in the library spaces and ask them to sign a release form to allow us to use their image. One of the benefits of owning your images is that you can make derivative works – you could try cropping and zooming into interesting details. For the Upgrade project I took dynamic pictures of our library users. I then gave them a cartoon effect in free software, cut the figures out of the background and put them on a one-colour background with a question in a strong font.

The addition of a QR Code allows the design to be more sparing while retaining a bit of mystery. Do you really need to mention every detail in your marketing materials? Could you add a URL or QR Code instead? By drawing people in with the marketing you could allow them to discover the product or service this way.

We have an archive in the library at City University which contains lots of photographs dating back to the early days of the institution. This is a really good way to get hold of images as they are free, unique and say something about your

Figure 3.1 *City University's Upgrade Project poster*

Figure 3.2 *City University's welcome poster*

institution. Because we own the pictures I chose to use for the new Help Desk signage, I could adapt them in Photoshop and re-colour them to give them an interesting retro feel that would fit in with newly refurbished space, which has a more traditional and scholarly feel. Even though the images are traditional, by reworking them the end product still has an element of fun – who doesn't like looking at the huge card catalogues of old?

When adapting images, remember to keep them in proportion – a stretched picture looks really unprofessional.

Software and professional printing

If you are intending to send your work to a commercial printer, it's a good idea to invest in some design software – I use Adobe Photoshop and Illustrator. Layout software such as InDesign or Quark Xpress is useful for designing publications such as multipage booklets. However, I have used a range of free online tools and Microsoft Publisher is also useful for layout. When preparing work for commercial printing, keep in mind that printers may ask for bleed, crop marks and for the work to be in CMYK colour format. Most printers usually accept work in PDF format and most have a list of terminology on their website if you need help deciphering 'print speak'.

Finding inspiration and developing concepts

Keep looking at stuff. Check out books on graphic design. I pick up leaflets, flyers and cards wherever I go and keep a scrap book. Look to inspirational institutions like museums and other libraries – what are they doing? It's good to get ideas and look at current trends to help stimulate your own original ideas. There are some really good graphic design blogs and Twitter feeds around, one of my favourites is the Spoon Graphics Blog by Chris Spooner (at www.blog.spoongraphics.co.uk). You can even find a lot of online tutorials which teach you step by step how to achieve some interesting effects. Exeriment with online tools for more inspiration: try Be Funky for photo effects (at www.befunky.com), Fotoflexer for image editing (at http://fotoflexer.com) and Inkscape, an open source graphics editor (at http://inkscape.org/).

Finally on the subject of design, an effective way to get the most from a marketing budget is to create your promotional materials with a view to re-using them in future campaigns. This basically means taking away any barriers there might be to re-use – don't put dates on posters or printed leaflets, or else they can really only be used in that year; in guides and brochures don't use screen-grabs of content that may significantly change or become unavailable in the near future.

You can also create promotional materials in such a way that they'll serve multiple uses. This is particularly true of presentations – if you're delivering a presentation about your library service, this can be broken down into several useful parts afterwards. For example, you can record yourself delivering the presentation and make the audio available as a downloadable podcast, you can take the main sections of your presentation and use them to create separate, more focused slide decks dotted around your website, and you can create a video version of the slides which you can then upload to YouTube and embed in your website (see 'Marketing with video' in Chapter 7).

If possible, film instructional videos in such a way that key content can be updated without having to start from scratch. For example, use screen-casting software to capture any use of the library catalogue or other systems, so that when these change and are updated these sections of film can easily be replaced with new ones. If you film the screen with a user in shot, you'll have to find the same user and re-shoot the entire sequence, costing time and money.

5 Make language a priority

The importance of using language your users understand, for all library materials, is something which cannot be overstated. Everyone knows plain, simple language is best and that jargon and acronym-heavy dirge should be avoided, but it's still a rule commonly ignored in libraries. It's crucial to put the effort in to align your language and vernacular with that of your members. Take a step back: would you know what terms like 'circulation', 'hold' and 'periodicals' meant if you weren't a library employee? There's not much wrong with 'loan', 'reservation' and 'journal'. In the past there may have been some gravitas in libraries giving learned, scholarly headings to things; those days are long gone. People want simple, clear instructions and titles.

User-testing to ensure that people understand the library's communication is always a good idea if time and budget allow, but evidence already exists that access to information can be inhibited by jargon, acronyms or over-complicated language. John Kupersmith (Reference Librarian at the University of California, Berkeley) has undertaken research in this area over a number of years – the key findings are these:

- The average success rate for finding journal articles or article databases is just 52% – Kupersmith cites library terminology as a major factor in this.
- The terms most often *not* understood by users are periodical, reference, resource, plus the usual acronyms and brand names.
- The terms most often *mis*understood by users are catalogue, database and e-journal.
- Electronic Resources is not a phrase that attracts users and encourages them to investigate further.

You can read more about his research at www.jkup.net/terms.html.

6 Write a manual

If you've gone to all the trouble of completing steps one to five, it'll all be for nothing if you don't make all the information readily available to everyone who needs it. A house style manual, well promoted and easy to find, is essential. Preferably combine this with part of the library's website or intranet which contains templates (for example for PowerPoint presentations, official letters etc.) and graphics (like the logo, in various different sizes and versions).

Related to this is the need to communicate successfully the brand's ideals and style to the staff who work in the library. Good buy-in is essential to a brand being applied all the way across a library service; staff are more inclined to this when they feel consulted, well informed and involved in the process.

Merchandise

Library merchandizing is perhaps an underexplored area. It goes against the traditionally passive nature of the library profession to think about putting the library's name on an object and selling it to the users. But, it can be a really useful marketing exercise – and even a revenue stream.

Things to buy

Libraries traditionally sell postcards, branded mugs, bookmarks and so on – but it is possible to be more ambitious and still be successful. If your library is of the 'beautiful and old' variety then an artfully shot calendar can earn back its costs quickly if promoted well.

The best merchandise takes the library brand and turns that into the selling point – it creates lifestyle products that continually remarket the library, rather than just providing some library revenue. In the second case study of the chapter, we'll look at one such success story, involving some bags, a stereotype and some aggressive marketing tactics.

Case study 5: Sshhh...! bags and library merchandise | Katy Sidwell

At the University of Leeds, library merchandizing was taken to eye-catching levels with the 'Sshhh...!' bags. Born of necessity (environmental policies in the wider University meaning the library could no longer offer plastic carrier bags to help students carry the books they borrowed) the small jute book-bags became something of an international success story, attracting coverage in the Guardian *newspaper among other media outlets.*

The idea was simple – the bags had 'Sshhh...!' written on the front, along with the library's website URL at the bottom, and the URL of the University's IT department on the back (as they helped fund the initial run of bags). They were cheap and came in a range of four bright colours. They tapped into the 'I am not a plastic bag' zeitgeist of the time, they provided a practical solution to carrying armfuls of books, and crucially they were desirable objects. People really wanted them (and indeed still do, at the time of writing) and at £5 for two, discerning students and staff could afford to indulge in a little completism by getting all the colours. When a run of colours had finished, a new colour was produced.

What really sets this apart from the usual 'bookmark with a logo on' style of library merchandizing are two things: firstly they transcended their status as 'library bags' to just become bags that people wanted to be seen holding, and secondly they were aggressively marketed. My personal favourite aspect of the way they were marketed is that each colour had only a limited run, to increase their value through scarcity. Once a run of bags had sold out, you could never get that colour again. This meant that a huge number of people have bought one of every single colour of the bag . . . A Facebook group sprang up, entitled 'I have a Sshhh . . .! bag therefore I am cool', and a website was created to track Sshhh...! bag sightings around the world – a map of sightings, with clickable links to Sshhh...! bags at the top of the Eiffel tower, or at the Taj Mahal. This is the kind of proactive marketing which libraries could successfully undertake, but seldom think to do.

Katy Sidwell is a subject librarian with a special interest in marketing and communications, which led her to achieve the CIM Professional Diploma in

Figure 3.3 *A Sshhh...! bag at the Taj Mahal, used with permission from Melissa Highton*

Marketing. She is now responsible for marketing at University of Leeds Library, alongside her subject role; she was behind the Sshhh...! bag design and production:

How did the idea first come about?

We were often asked for bags by customers with a pile of books they had just borrowed and nothing to carry them in – we used a pile of recycled plastic bags from supermarkets and then we got some sponsorship to put our own identity on new plastic bags. We weren't happy about the environmental consequences of this and we were looking for a sustainable and green alternative. We spotted Jutexpo, the jute bags supplier, at a conference, and when we got back we managed to persuade the library to invest in them. To make the bags affordable we had to buy in bulk, so this wasn't a trivial amount of money, given that we hadn't sold goods like this before and were unsure of the market. The Sshhh...! idea came out of a Marketing Group meeting, where the initial colours were also agreed.

Roughly how many have been sold in total now?
Between 2006 and mid-2011 we have sold over 35,000 bags – approximately, because we have also given some away as induction freebies at the start of the academic year. There was a boom after they were first introduced, which has now settled down to a slower but steady sales rate.

And do you make a profit on the bags?
We don't aim to make a big profit on the bags – we don't want to fleece library customers! – just enough to buy the next lot and leave a small margin.

Tell us about limiting the colour-runs to increase desirability . . .
This was a decision made early on – as soon as we realized the bags were selling like hot cakes. It seemed an obvious and easy product development angle and there was a thought that a core market might want to collect each colour as it came out! We also tried to balance the colour options (we usually get two colours in one batch) so one was bright and one was more muted, with an eye to the masculine as well as feminine (although they're predominantly bought by women, men do use them as well).

Have you introduced any variations to the range?
We stuck with different block colours for quite a while, but have also introduced a 'mini-Sshhh...! ' bag on two occasions as special editions, the latest to celebrate the 75th anniversary of the Brotherton Library opening. We've moved on to a mix of colours with a two-tone and spotted version in the latest batch. We're considering developments like longer handles, although this adds to the cost, and I would love to run a design competition for students to create a new look for the bags.

What has been the effect of the bags on the library generally?
It's a real buzz to see Sshhh...! bags out and about – I've spotted them up and down the country and we created a community map online where people could post photos of bags in exotic places – we're only missing Antarctica now I think! (Trying to ignore the irony of the environmentally-conscious bag having such appalling air miles.)

Getting national (Guardian) and local (Yorkshire Evening Post) press coverage for such a positive thing is great. It is a fun element to our normal business that students have engaged with – as well as the Facebook group created by students there was an article in the student newspaper declaring it 'the new Louis

Vuitton'! We've also worked with other university departments to create one-off variations for events and conferences. It's certainly a very visible profile-raiser around the university and probably our most successful marketing venture in terms of impact and longevity.

There is a school of thought that we should never indulge in library stereotypes, even if we treat them playfully or otherwise try to undermine them, because they are perpetuated through use. Do you have any worries about the fact that such a library success story relies on the old shushing cliché?
If you can't beat 'em, join 'em, but at least do it creatively and ironically! Changing stereotypes is incredibly difficult – especially when some of them are borne out by personal experience – have you ever been 'shushed' in a library or witnessed it happening? It happens – even if it's not always the librarians doing it. These strong simplifications and distortions will remain in the public consciousness no matter how careful we are in our use of vocabulary and images. Sometimes strenuously protesting against stereotypes can come across as precious and lacking in self-confidence – embrace it and enjoy subverting it in a creative way: shout Sshhh...! proudly from the rooftops!

If you are marketing you need to communicate quickly – within a few seconds. We wanted something recognizably 'library' but also not obviously so – in order that students could carry it about town as something attractive in its own right. In short, it's worked for us.

Give-aways

Free pens are ubiquitous. Everyone seems to be giving away pens with their logo on these days, from banks to charities to publishers. The reason pens are such good tools for promotion is because firstly they have intrinsic usefulness, and secondly ownership of them is transient. We use them all the time, we borrow them all the time, and we don't always give them back. Unlike a flyer or a leaflet, our interest in them doesn't end as soon as we've used them once. They don't get thrown out straightaway or filed and forgotten about. Chances are the first person who makes use of your free library pen will be an existing user – the promotional benefit of this will be to reward them for their patronage, making them feel good towards the library, and to remind them, next time they write something down, that they must visit their excellent library again. But later on that pen may change hands and a whole new audience is met with information about your library; apparently, pens are often used by up to ten people in their lifetime. Obvious avenues for disseminating free branded merchandise are trade shows or employment fairs, and in packs at conferences, but it's nice to have a supply of pens available at the issue and reference desks – that way when someone asks to borrow a pen, you can say 'here, have this one to keep'. Pens are relatively low cost and if even one person joins the library for every 100 pens you give out, that's a great return.

With all free branded items, the idea is to make them recognizably the library's, to give people something to think about, and to facilitate their finding further information. So while the name of the library on the side of a pen or a bookmark is fine, it could be better to include a message to get people to engage (like 'Get free stuff! Come to the library!'), and then a simple URL in case the user wants to follow up – www.nameofyourlibrary.com/offer for example, could take them to a page aimed at enticing new users via the library's 'offer'.

If you have more budget to spend on merchandise, USB memory sticks have all sorts of marketing potential. Like the pens they are fairly universally useful, and easy to brand with your library's visual identity. But unlike pens, they can be loaded with promotional materials. If you are running a course that involves computers, or social media, or Web 2.0, then send all those registered on the course a memory stick with the training materials included, along with useful online bookmarks, and library brochures, posters, guides and so on. You could even include an MP3 of a podcast highlighting other relevant courses they may wish to attend.

Slogans

The use of a slogan to market a library moves closer to the world of traditional advertising than is the case with most of the contents of this book. It's certainly not somewhere every library will want to go so I won't cover it in detail here, but for some public libraries in particular it can be very effective – if it makes clear *why the library will benefit the user*.

It might be that a suitable slogan is right under your nose, as Francisco Dao (2006) points out: 'The criteria for a good mission statement and a good marketing slogan are also the same. Both should be unequivocally clear in communicating the company's goals and proposition.' So if your library's mission statement leans towards the direct rather than the unfocused, it might provide either the slogan itself or the inspiration to create one.

My personal opinion is that discretion should be the better part of valour in this area, and that libraries should only be marketing with a slogan if it's a *really* good one. One such example is Calgary Public Library, which uses the slogan 'Everything You're Into' in conjunction with brilliant marketing campaigns to illustrate how the library has resources to meet everyone's needs.

Figures 3.4 and 3.5 are two examples of how the slogan was used. The first is coffee sleeves featuring the slogan, and the second shows one of many advertisements placed in grocery stores, themed to suit the items surrounding them.

Figure 3.4 *Calgary Public Library's coffee sleeve advertising*

Grant Kaiser, Manager of Marketing, explains the thinking behind the campaign:

> One of the great challenges in marketing libraries is overcoming people's usually outdated understanding of what a library is and does. The "Everything You're Into" campaign was designed to catch people off guard, and get them thinking differently about the library and the role it could play in their lives. Messages were deliberately positioned in unexpected places, such as in grocery stores, on

Figure 3.5 *Calgary Public Library's banana advertising*

coffee cups, on the side of a bus, and even pressure-washed into sidewalks. The community reaction was overwhelmingly positive, and was gauged through before and after public opinion surveying. Customers loved that the library was showing itself to be alive, approachable, and creative, making them proud of an organization they love. Non-users reported seeing the library as a more modern, positive, and "mainstream" organization. Both groups reported seeing the library as a more relevant part of their lives after experiencing the campaign.

Proof, then, that in the right circumstances the aggressive tactics of traditional marketing – slogans, advertising, guerrilla stunts like marketing via washable graffiti – can be successful in the library environment.

Branding and marketing a converged library and IT service

Converged and superconverged services are increasingly prevalent for libraries, particularly in higher education. From a branding perspective this presents an obvious challenge, in that two or more existing brands may have to come together to form one new brand, in addition to which there may be a requirement for them to retain some individual branding at the same time. A co-operative approach is essential between the two or more divisions of the converged service, as is an overall guiding hand to unite the service – in effect, a merged IT and library service has to market itself collectively *and* its component parts individually.

Stephen Pinfield, Chief Information Officer for the University of Nottingham, provides the final case study of this chapter. Nottingham have been operating converged IT, library, archive and media services since 2002, across all of its university campuses – not just in the UK but in China and Malaysia as well.

Case study 6: Marketing a converged service | Stephen Pinfield

When a service first converges, how important is it to 'launch' the new system with a big rebranding, bells and whistles promotion and so on?
Information Service (IS) at Nottingham has always focused on marketing its *services* rather than marketing *itself*. Marketing activity is therefore specifically designed to be as user-focused as possible, relating to the needs of different

groups of users at different times. Induction material for students, for example, covers the key things that students need to know during their first few weeks at the University (logging into the student network service, finding material in the library, and so on), rather than telling them about IS as a department.

That having been said, as part of the 2002 restructuring, IS did develop a new corporate identity, including a new logo, to replace the identities of the previously separate departments. The new logo was used in signage and marketing collateral until 2009. In that year IS, like all other units in the University, dropped separate logos and adopted the University corporate identity.

That change marked a significant transition in the marketing set up at Nottingham – a move towards much greater co-ordination of marketing and communication activity across different units in the institution. This meant, for example, that induction material for students was presented in integrated publications in a more holistic way for the University as a whole. There is now little or no distinction between services provided by IS and those of other departments in the induction information. The emphasis is on the student experience, not the organizational structure of the service departments of the University.

Marketing and communications, however, have always been and remain important to IS. The economies of scale associated with convergence in 2002, enabled IS to have the capacity to appoint a specialized marketing professional to co-ordinate marketing and communication activities. In 2010, the bold step was taken of moving what was by then an IS marketing and communications team into the University Communications and Marketing department. This coincided with the more co-ordinated approach to marketing and communications across the institution. Although these staff continue to work mainly on IS-related activities, they are now embedded amongst other marketing professionals.

This move was undoubtedly a risk, since there was a danger that the team would lose its focus, and therefore needed to be managed carefully. But it does create the potential for a more co-ordinated, institutional approach to marketing IS services. The emphasis is on IS and its services being an integral part of the institution and as a central component of the overall University experience for students and staff.

Have you found any techniques or strategies particularly useful in marketing your converged service, which weren't so pertinent when you were marketing 'just' a library?
One debate we have had at Nottingham over the years has been the extent to which we use the word 'library' or not. Currently, we use 'library' to describe buildings, we have sections of our organization that are labelled 'library' (such as

Library Customer Services), and we use generic terms such as 'digital library services'. However, we do not have a department called the 'Library'.

'Library' undoubtedly has strong brand recognition – and generally a positive one. However, there is a great deal of evidence to suggest that users understand the word in quite narrow terms. To many users, 'the library' is a physical building. It is common, for example, to hear academic staff say that they do not use the library, by which they mean they do not visit the physical building. They do, of course, use library services online, but interestingly often do not associate these digital services with 'the library'. This is a perception issue that many library services experience.

For a converged service this should not be a big problem since it will be generally understood that the Information Services department will be responsible for digital services. However, there is a danger that the positive aspects of the term 'library' begin to disappear with the emphasis on a converged Information Services, and this can lead to some brand recognition problems. A balance needs to be achieved between on the one hand use of the word 'library' in order to connect with users, and on the other hand acknowledgement that library services are more than just about a physical building.

How important is it that the users properly understand what constitutes the service? Do they need to understand that it is one holistic department to get the most out of it, or can they simply engage with the parts relevant to them and ignore the cogs that come together to turn the wheels?
One of the major aims of convergence of Nottingham was to create a more joined-up user experience of information and technology services which did not require users to understand the organizational structures of the service department. The aim was that services should be provided in a transparent way, and the ability of users to get the best out of them should not rely on them understanding how the department is managed.

When a student has a query about accessing a reading list in the University virtual learning environment, is that a library problem or learning technology problem? When a member of staff has a problem with their password when using an e-journal, is that an IT problem or a library problem? In both cases, the users should not have to know which service department can help solve their problem, rather they should just be able to get the problem sorted quickly.

From a customer point of view then, users should not have to understand anything about the structure of the information and technology services department in order to consume its services on a day-to-day basis. Contact and liaison structures, including a single IT helpline, should be set up to enable users to consume services and sort out problems quickly and easily.

In other ways, however, it is important that some people outside the converged department do understand the organizational structure. This applies particularly to those involved in planning services or liaising with IS regarding the development of strategy. Here it is important to understand enough about the structure to know who to contact. At more senior levels of the institution, therefore, it is essential that there is an awareness of the structures of the IS department to enable useful partnership working.

In my experience, the larger an organization, the harder it is to be agile. The ability to be flexible and respond to change quickly is pretty essential in marketing – how does one maintain that agility in a converged service?
Creating an organization that can deliver reliable core services and at the same time generate innovation is a real challenge. Innovation is certainly an essential feature of an IS department but it does create risk. It is, therefore, inappropriate to give the same emphasis to innovation in all areas of the service, particularly those areas where robust and reliable services are the highest priority. It is important to identify strategically *which* areas of the Department's remit need to major on innovation and focus on ensuring that *those* areas are sufficiently agile.

Giving staff the time and the space to spot opportunities and communicate ideas, and then the ability to experiment and take risks, are all important aspects of innovation. This can be enabled by encouraging project-based, cross-team working and developing a culture of ideas-generation.

Finally, is there a danger that we end up spending all our energy on marketing the concept of a converged service, and not marketing the actual services we provide at all . . .?
This is definitely a danger. But it would be a big mistake to fall into this. You do, however, have to be aware of how the Department as a whole is perceived and make efforts to ensure this is as positive as possible. But it is important to recognize that the best way to achieve a positive image is to do a good job.

For too long libraries have been unconcerned with branding, but this area is no longer one we can afford to ignore. Libraries must be run like successful businesses in order to thrive and to continue to have sufficient support from their internal stakeholders. Further reading and additional information can be found at **www.librarymarketingtoolkit.com/p/library-brand.html.**

CHAPTER 4

Marketing and the library building

Library design

Very closely related to the branding issues discussed in the previous chapter is the layout and presentation of the library building itself – the Physical Evidence from Booms and Bitner's Seven Ps of marketing (see page 7). Good library design is perfectly possible without dramatic spaces and breathtaking architecture, and stems from seeing the library through a user's eyes rather than a librarian's eyes. James Neal, Vice President for Information Services and University Librarian at Columbia University, puts it best – he allowed me to quote him here: 'Start with the user, not with the collection. Start with the technology and not with the staff.' That is the key to designing the library's interior in such a way as to enhance the user experience.

Unlike much of the material in this book, the design of the library is potentially a costly area of marketing. With that in mind, the focus should be on determining the value libraries get from redesigning their premises, and rebranding themselves with new names and identities – an aspect of library marketing which has had greatly increased prominence in the last decade or so. It has become an accepted part of the process of communicating the fact that libraries are changing, with patrons and potential patrons whose perceptions of the library may be some years, or even decades, behind the reality. But does this process yield tangible results? Is there a return on the investment of redesign?

The second case study of the chapter goes a long way to answering that question. Fiona Williams is the Head of Libraries and Heritage at City of York Council, and was responsible for overseeing the transformation of York's main library (and a number of regional branches) into 'Explore Library Learning Centres'. She talks about the logistics of redesigning and refurbishing a public library, the process of marketing the change, and how the results have impacted on use of the library.

First of all, though, we hear from Kevin Hennah, a library design consultant from Australia. Although visual identity is most commonly associated with materials (publicity materials, user guides, presentation materials and so on) it also applies to the building, and the first case study in this chapter explores this area in more detail.

Case study 7: Library design and visual merchandizing | Kevin Hennah

Kevin Hennah is a library Consultant, trainer and public speaker who works throughout Australia and internationally. He is the author of Public Libraries Image Handbook (2005), and works with School, Public, University and Special Libraries on interior design, shoestring makeovers, and developing marketing strategies for print materials in the internet age. I started off by asking him about visual merchandizing.

Why is visual identity and branding so important in marketing libraries?

Visual identity or image is becoming increasingly important to most businesses and organizations. Reflect on what you considered acceptable standards of presentation in retail, hospitality, tourism, cafés and restaurants 10–20 years ago in contrast to your expectations today. Businesses are setting higher standards and this generates higher expectations. Take the retail industry, for example. Most shopping centres insist their tenants carry out a total shop refit every 5 years to ensure presentations standards are consistently high. The hard bench seats in the shopping mall of ten or so years ago have been replaced with comfortable lounges. Screens are replacing posters. Marketing strategies are becoming more sophisticated. Quite simply, image drives perception and libraries also need to keep up to date. Especially if they are to attract a younger audience.

In addition, I believe there should be a level of uniformity across a library network. Particularly across a public library service. I am in full support of tailoring the design, decor and collection to the local demographic. However, I am referring to branding. That is, taking a uniform approach to all signage and print collateral. It not only looks professional, but also it helps build presence in the community and reinforces that the group of libraries work together. This is a fundamental principle of marketing and promotion.

External signage is also critical. I have often joked with my clients that the most effective way to find a public library is to look for heavily tinted windows that are covered with paper signs, Blu-Tack and Sellotape and of course, a distinct absence of external signage. Libraries need to take ownership of their space and ensure the signage demands the public's attention from all angles.

One of the key ideas I'd like to emphasize is most libraries have failed to develop a visual merchandizing strategy to help print compete with new technologies. In the design and renovation process, much effort is invested in architecture and decor (which I see as very important); however this is often an exciting veneer around an outdated visual merchandizing strategy for the collection itself.

Let's talk about practical steps to take. How can we improve the library space to better market the library?
While public libraries are often better at weeding, very few have explored exciting new ways to showcase the collection. Sometimes in fear of negative feedback from the elderly – yet at the same time, turning a blind eye to the fact that they fail to attract a younger audience. Public libraries should avoid large seating zones that feel like doctors' waiting rooms! Instead, create an inviting community lounge, with a variety of seating types for groups as well as individuals who wish to read or use a laptop.

Some public libraries are still building 'Titanic' service desks alongside self-check terminals; this is as good as saying 'don't bother'! All libraries should create a flexible environment by putting as much as possible on wheels, especially shelving. Lower, movable shelving may require weeding. However, 80% of loans are generated by only 20% of the collection.

For print to compete with new technologies it is essential that libraries use plenty of front-facing shelves, as book covers are a powerful 'selling' tool and help to 'punctuate' rows of spines. Take a lead from retail, which has front-facing books on all bay ends. This is excellent promotional space and it looks much more attractive than pin boards covered in signs.

So should libraries be trying to think more like the retail market? What else can we learn from non-library marketing?
There is an enormous amount that libraries can learn from retail. For example, first impressions count; if a retailer fails to create an exciting first impression, they'll most likely fail. The entrance of a library should be very similar. I like to see powerful features of front-faced resources around themes such as 'Quick Pick', 'In the Media', 'Just Returned' and 'What's Hot'. Unfortunately, many libraries are still allocating this prime real estate to photocopiers, freestanding pin boards or worse still, a book sale trolley.

Inexperienced retailers often believe the more stock they hold, the greater their sales potential. This is not the case. Of course you need depth and variety to be credible. However, powerful merchandizing in both retail book stores and libraries is about striking the balance between volume and also allocating space to what I refer to as 'hero walls', impulse stands and feature bays. A successful retailer or library understands that visual merchandizing is a silent sales person and a great deal of consideration needs to be invested in placing the right collection, in the right volume at the right time and of course, with the right signage!

Can you tell us about a specific library you've worked on redesigning, and what effect your work has had?
I receive e-mails on a weekly basis from libraries that have actioned ideas they picked up in my consultations, presentations and workshops – simple and often inexpensive initiatives to increase usage and loans.

One of my favourite was from an academic library. Realizing that row after row of spine-out books was no longer the best strategy, they decided to remove anything that had not been borrowed in the past two years. At the same time, they placed a short-term hold on buying books and allocated their budget to front-facing shelves. These shelves were used to draw attention to resources they had previously purchased and had not been borrowed.

The weed represented 30% of the collection. Loans instantly increased by 50%! I was also amused to hear that they received comments along the lines of 'It's great to see the library are finally buying some new books!'

I'm not suggesting that this percentage or this result will translate to all libraries, but I do find most libraries compromise visual merchandizing standards in order to achieve volume – a volume that is often totally underutilized.

How much should library design be based on general principles, and how much should it be based on the specific demographic or community that the library is aimed at?
The foundations of my ideas translate to almost all libraries. For example, we need to build flexible spaces. All shelving and as much furniture as possible should be on wheels so that staff can massage layout in line with changing statistics, needs and of course developments in technology.

My bigger picture ideas on visual merchandizing strategy also translate. However, demographics will steer how much space is allocated to each collection and how many front-facing books I would recommend. An academic library may choose to have fewer front-facing books than a library that has a browsing collection. Some libraries can justify a reasonably large print reference collection while others may interfile with non-fiction.

I also think there is merit in setting the library up around genres in certain demographics. Some go as far as to merge fiction and non-fiction together and create genre-based lounges. As such, the resources are grouped according to content, not what they physically are. So for example, if someone is interested in history, they will find books on World Wars alongside Historical Fiction, Biography, DVDs and Antique Magazines. I'm not prescribing this for all libraries, but I know of one library that implemented this and experienced a 22% increase in loans. Obviously it worked for their community.

Is there one idea or concept that can guide all our decisions about how to set up the library?
My golden rule for setting up, merchandizing and managing a library is: how would you set up this library if you were to get a dollar in your personal bank account for every item borrowed? What would you change? Most people answer 'everything!'

Essentially every resource and piece of furniture must 'pay the rent' of the space it occupies.

For more information on Kevin Hennah, visit www.kevinhennah.com.au.

Signs and displays

Following on from what Kevin says above, signs and displays still play a vital role. There is a lot of emphasis in these pages on new ways to market the library; however this doesn't mean the old ways don't have value, and a well put-together display of books can still increase circulation.

David Lee King (who provides a case study in the next chapter) works at Topeka and Shawnee County Public Library. They took an innovative approach to boosting the circulation of oft-overlooked titles: librarians Michelle Eklund and Jennifer Jones created a display of wrapped books, whose covers had been obscured and replaced with a few hand-written keywords. Customers responded well to the invitation to take a chance . . . (Read more at: www.tscpl.org/books-movies-music/innovative-book-display-puts-covers-under-wraps.) There are plenty of opportunities for public libraries (and, to an extent, further and higher education libraries) to tie in displays with cultural events attracting coverage in the national or local news.

Figure 4.1 *TSCPL's Wrapped books display (photo by Lissa Stanley)*

Signage is a huge part of marketing which is all too often overlooked. Clear and friendly signs make an enormous difference to the user experience, and a lack of clear and friendly signs can make the user feel angry or stupid. Libraries are in the slightly awkward position of having to communicate a lot of information that is prohibitive in some way – 'please don't use your mobile here', 'please don't return books here' and so on. This is sometimes unavoidable but the negative effects can be mitigated by (a) being friendly and conversational about it, (b) putting in some positive signs that tell people when they *can* do things and most importantly (c) making it clear where the customer can go to fulfil their needs. No 'out-of-order' sign should ever go up without a note at the bottom telling the customer where the nearest equivalent self-issue machine/toilet/photocopier is. If you're trying to encourage self-issue, then a sign at the desk saying it is not for borrowing or returning books must be accompanied by clear directions to the nearest machines that facilitate this.

Marketing the library as space

As libraries change to become more like modern bookshops (just as bookshop chains are failing), so they become a much more attractive space in which just to *be*. Research conducted by the Museums, Libraries and Archives Council (MLA, 2010) asked respondents what would encourage them to visit the library and what would discourage them. Interestingly, 'Having a coffee shop on site' scored highest as a positive, with 32% saying this would encourage them to visit – but it was also second highest as a negative (behind only 'None of these') with 23% choosing it as the factor that would most discourage a library visit. This neatly encapsulates the tension between what libraries used to do, and how this is valued by certain sections of society; and what they are increasingly doing now, and how this in turn is valued by other sections of society.

Nevertheless, coffee shops on site are increasingly common and despite many people both inside and outside the profession having reservations about the idea, it seems more people want them than don't. The second and third most popular things to encourage library use were 'Activities for children and families' (27% chose that) and 'Longer opening hours, e.g. evenings and weekends' (26%) – both of these support the notion that the library should be marketed as a space and a place to go, not just as a building full of books and other scholarly or fun resources ('Improving the range/quality of books' came in fourth in the poll, with 21% of people choosing it).

Marketing the library as space means producing promotional materials (leaflets, posters, online campaigns etc.) which focus on the assets of the building and the space (rather than the collections) and disseminating them in new areas. This can mean anything from asking to put leaflets in a children's day-care centre (perhaps offering them something reciprocal, such as putting their own leaflets in the library) to tweeting when it is raining, as the British Library often does, something like: 'It's pouring outside – why not come in and use our free Wi-Fi till it clears up?'

Many redesigns and/or rebranding exercises are based around marketing the library as space to those who want to use it as space, and marketing the library as scholarly resource to those who want to use it as scholarly resource. Like so much we've already covered, it's an extremely tricky balance to get right.

Case study 8: Redesign and refurbishment | Fiona Williams

York Central Library became York Explore Library Learning Centre (known more colloquially as just 'York Explore') in May 2010, when it re-opened after a £540,000 redesign and refurbishment. It is my local library so I'm well placed to assess the 'before' and the 'after' – the difference is amazing. In particular the new entrance lobby, with three huge double-door openings leading off a central atrium, and not a gate, turnstile, barrier or even a reference desk in sight, is a revelation. It's hard to describe just how welcoming and accessible it feels.

The concept of Explore Library Learning Centres had been in development by City of York Council Libraries and Adult and Community Education for some time; the first and second examples had already opened in suburbs of the city of York in 2008. The central York Explore was funded in partnership with Aviva, the insurance giant whose offices back onto the local River Ouse. The key features of the Explore experience are a library with learning rooms, a crèche and café.

From a marketing perspective, rebranding is a huge exercise involving a lot of time and money, so if you're doing this at your own library you want to see a real return on your investment. For York Explore the numbers certainly support this. According to Helen Whitehead, Performance and Projects Manager, visits are 15% up on the previous version of the library. The momentum of the redesign means that, three years after opening, their target is to have a footfall of 1 million per annum, putting York Explore in the national top six busiest libraries. Book issues are 16% up on the previous year. Circulation of children's books has particularly increased – they have a new space, an extended range of related activities, and a simpler categorization system – with fiction up 59% and non-

fiction up 45%. Overall, in the first 9 months after re-opening, more than 11,000 new members have joined.

A survey undertaken in the library revealed some interesting results about why people liked the redesign. One new user said: 'I think that since Borders closed there has been a gap in the market for somewhere to have a coffee and browse books. I will definitely return', which certainly supports the idea of marketing the library as space. Another said simply 'It's all about the free Wi-Fi, baby!' This seems flippant and perhaps disappointing given all the investment in books, e-resources, architecture and so on – but it reveals an important truth, that libraries are providing many services to users now, all of which are valid and important. Whatever increases use is a good thing at a time when so many libraries are threatened.

Here is how Fiona Williams, Head of Libraries and Heritage at City of York Council, described the York Explore project.

Let's begin by covering the logistics of the refurbishment. What did members of the library do while it was closed, and what happened to the staff?

1 We extended the opening hours at other libraries.
2 Staff worked across the service. This both helped the branches and let central staff see the different experience that branch work is. There was also a training programme for staff and they all got together once a week at Explore Acomb to keep the sense of 'team' together.
3 The mobile library visited the city centre at the weekend. We decided against setting up a temporary library in the centre due to cost – we wanted to put all our investment into the transformation.
4 We moved key reference tools to other libraries or to the city archive – some people requested access to specific items e.g. old local newspapers, so we were able to ensure they were available.
5 Leading up to the closure we allowed the public to take as many books as they wanted and the loan period was for the duration of the closure. This was very popular and by the time we closed the shelves were all but bare – especially in the nonfiction. This meant we had less to pack and store! But equally it really caught people's imagination and has got me thinking about experimenting with loan periods.

I understand the new design has enabled around 200,000 extra books, *and* is a more flexible space with learning rooms and so on . . . How is that possible?

Figure 4.2 *The main entrance of York Explore. Image courtesy of Furmoto*

The building was designed as a library in 1927 by local architect Walter Brierley. Over the intervening years we had filled it with clutter, putting in partition walls to create office space. We emptied the building, took down all partition walls and brought two back rooms into use as public space. The principle was that space in the city centre is too valuable to use as offices or storage so all space was to be public space (apart from two offices for staff). It is a beautiful building with lots of natural light and space – we simply recreated that. Most comments reflect on the natural light and space, with some people asking if we have put in more windows!

I'm fascinated by the new entrance hall. The fact that there are no barriers or turnstiles, or even an issues desk overlooking the doorways, feels incredibly liberating for me as a user. Was the layout a deliberate attempt to make the library feel welcoming and all-encompassing or something more prosaic and practical than that?
It was deliberate. The old library was difficult to get into and a bit scary for a lot of people. It always reminded me of Alice in Wonderland, with all the doors saying 'No, you can't come through here'. The barriers were all for the benefit of the staff and the message we were giving was 'You are not trusted' and 'Libraries

are scary places'.

A key feature of an Explore Centre is a transition space – somewhere that you can walk into, understand the building and feel welcome and safe. Retail now have their tills at the back of shops with staff welcoming you. We wanted to replicate this approach. There are still far too many rules in libraries!

There are no security gates and no alarms, yet I'm told you haven't had a rise in book theft – is that right?

It is – people respond well to being trusted. The security is provided in a different way to barriers and alarms. It's through the staff being out and about and engaging with the public. Also, more people around means it's harder for people to steal. By creating a secure atmosphere and being aware of what is happening, we can ensure the safety of the books.

The reservations shelf isn't staffed – patrons can just pick their books up, identified by a label tied round them, and check them out. The potential for library anarchy here is enough to give most information professionals heart palpitations and yet, again, I'm told this system is working really well. Can you talk a little about this?

When I first came to York the requests were behind the counter and were filed by the date order when the postcard telling the person the book was in was sent out. So if you didn't have the postcard with you it was very difficult to find the book! It seemed madness to me. I had heard of other places which just put out the books alphabetically by surname and so we tried it and it works. It's all about what is easiest for the customer – and saving time for the staff. We need to reduce the amount of time they spend on straightforward things so they can spend more time helping people to discover new authors or read stories in the children's area.

Do you have any advice for other libraries that are working with architects, contractors, and other third parties?

Be clear about who is doing what and respect other specialisms. Our architect chose the colour, which I hated initially, but he knows about colour – I know about libraries. The colour is now perfect and I can see how and why it works. Just good communication and relentlessly pursuing the vision – never being deterred – holding the line – all those things really.

During the refurbishment and redesign, how did you keep local people informed? Was the local media important in this?

We worked with the council's marketing and communications dept throughout. We used our website and all our other libraries to let people know what was happening. I would do this better next time as I think we didn't do as much as we could have. We sent a brochure to every household when we re-opened – but I don't think it had much impact and I wouldn't do it again.

People often associate adding PCs and other multimedia equipment, even self-issue machines, with a reduction in book stock. Did you have any issues with this and how did you get the message across that modernization doesn't necessarily result in fewer books on the shelves?
Yes, we do have issues in this area. It's the constant struggle of explaining that it's not having lots of books that is important; it's what those books are and how they are used. We moved the reference section downstairs and interfiled the books with the lending stock to create one adult non-fiction run. So many reference tools are now available online and we are working to get that message across.

We do find, though, that most people understand this and prefer the new way. It is also bringing people back to the libraries – people who didn't think it was relevant to them. These are often people using the free Wi-Fi with their laptops.

People love the self-issue – I was very surprised at how quickly it was adopted by everyone. We talk about libraries being the gateway to the world's knowledge and ideas and the way to these is changing. Also the Explore Centres are not just libraries now – they are places where lots of different things happen as well.

What was the initial response from the community when you announced plans for the refurb, and what has been their response now they've actually seen and experienced it?
We had a lot of worried people. People who had used the library all their lives and were worried that we would destroy the building and make it too modern. This has changed since we re-opened. We have had a lot of comments from people who said they were expecting to hate it – but they love it. People were especially worried about the café – but again they love it and they use it lots.

I think a lot of people saw it was time for a change and were pleased with the outcome. As the original architect, Walter Brierley, was a local man and it is a listed [protected] building, we worked hard to ensure that we respected the building and worked with it to create the new spaces.

Finally let's discuss the mechanics of marketing. How does York Explore market itself, and how has this changed since the redesign?

It's about getting the customer experience right. We're still in the early days really and are working with Aviva, learning lots from their marketing expertise. We are using their 'message houses', which turn around everything to the viewpoint of people – staff, customers, stakeholders. So we're learning to think what we want customers to say about their experience – a customer-first approach.

We are using social media more now – Facebook and Twitter. This is helping us to think about the language and approach we use in marketing which in the past has been perhaps a little stilted. We market the centre in terms of what you can do there e.g. family history, reading, learning and as a destination in itself. We are open in the evening and are trying to grow that business – York tends to be a bit quiet after 6 p.m., so we're thinking about how we fit into the evening economy. For families we are the key place to come in the early evening – have a light tea, etc. And we're a safe place to meet for people who don't want to go to a pub.

A big change is that people are doing our marketing for us as well – word of mouth is being hugely influential in increasing use. Our chief executive challenges staff who haven't been spreading the word, and everywhere I go people tell me how much they love it. I go everywhere telling people about it and make sure it is on everyone's radar.

Do you have one top tip or guiding principle when it comes to promoting the library service?
Have a clear vision and keep the message simple.

This case study shows that the benefits of rebranding and redesigning are tangible and real, which is encouraging for libraries when most media coverage of rebranding often focuses on people complaining about the new name. Further reading, including some additional material from Fiona Williams about York Explore and their rebranding, can be found at **www.librarymarketingtoolkit.com/p/marketing-and-library-building.html**.

CHAPTER 5
An introduction to online marketing

There now follows a suite of three related chapters all about the internet in its various manifestations, and using it to market successfully. Although Chapters 6 and 7 deal with more advanced Web 2.0 concepts, it would be wrong to describe this introduction to online marketing as 'the basics' – it's more like the fundamentals. As such, case study contributions are of a particularly 'how-to' bent in this chapter: David Lee King gives seven top tips for the library website, Aaron Tay details the importance of a library presence on mobile devices, and Alison Wallbutton gives advice on how to market with e-mail.

The library website

Despite the emergence of Web 2.0 applications and social media activities (which we shall get onto later) the library's main website is still an absolutely essential marketing tool for several reasons. Most obviously, library website use is up exponentially for most libraries in the last few years. Users and potential users will be Googling your library, so what they find online will make a huge difference as to whether they then visit your premises in person.

Physical footfall is simply no longer fit for purpose as a measure of a library's success, because so much can be done online – every book renewal or reservation made using the internet is a visit to the library building saved. Often the media – and perhaps those holding the purse-strings for libraries – will take a reduction in footfall as proof that a library is no longer being used as much, making it a soft target for cuts. It's vital that in marketing libraries, to both internal and external stakeholders, that we emphasize the compound number of visits – physical and online combined. The Chartered Institute of Public Finance and Accountancy conducted a survey (CIPFA, 2010) about library use in the UK during the preceding five years. Physical attendance was found to be down by around 4%; online activity was up by a massive 49% across the country in the last year alone. As discussed above, this would more than account for the drop in footfall – in fact, one could interpret the statistics as representing an overall increase in the use of libraries. The compound figure of physical visits and library website visits has increased by 34 million from 2007/08 to 2008/09. So in other words: people are using the library websites more and more, and to waste that marketing opportunity would be a real shame.

Online, everything happens very quickly. People will scan the main sections of a page rather than read in depth, and make a decision within *three seconds* as to whether they want to stay on that page or move on. If they do decide to stay, they pay most attention to the content in the top part of the screen – this must contain some really arresting words or images that tempt them to investigate further, therefore. A huge, static logo is not desirable here, and nor is lots of complicated text about the library – that's effectively dead space and so not maximizing your visitors' attention. In actual fact, keeping things simple and striking in this part of the site can serve as an example to the rest of it, too – as Alison Circle (featured in Chapter 2) says: 'In today's world people can only absorb simple, clear messages. Don't tell them everything. They don't care.'

The first case study is simple and to the point: David Lee King, Digital Branch Manager for Topeka and Shawnee County Public Library in the USA, describes the seven essential elements for a great library website. David is a leading figure in libraries online, he has published his own book about web design, *Designing the Digital Experience* (King, 2008), and his library's website is a fantastic example of how it *should* be done: have a look for yourself at www.tscpl.org. Note the dynamic content in that key area at the top of the screen, engaging the user straight away.

Case study 9: The seven essential elements to an awesome library website | David Lee King

When I started creating this list, I figured I would list out things like 'library catalogue' or 'locations and hours'. And I did, in fact, list out the catalogue first. Then it dawned on me: the catalogue itself isn't an essential part – the catalogue leads to the essential stuff a library has . . . the actual resources.

With that type of thinking in mind, here are the essential elements to a library website:

1 Customers want something to read, watch, and listen to when they visit the library. Obviously libraries need a library catalogue. But that doesn't satisfy the immediate need of our customers, does it? They came to read. So why not meet that need? Create a new books blog with book reviews, or even news of the library (if it's interesting). Our customers are into media in many formats, so why not meet that need too? Create a podcast, and make some fun how-to videos that can be viewed at the website. Why not have a story time or two for the kids, while you're at it?

2 Customers have questions, and come to the library for answers. We can provide that too, through comments on blog posts, an 'ask a librarian' e-mail/Instant Messaging/text messaging service, and even by providing a phone number on the website.

3 Customers need to know the normal stuff, too. So provide basic information like how to get a library card, hours, locations and a map of the building.

4 Websites need actual staff! A website meeting the needs listed above, needs actual staff to do the actual work. It's a library, after all. Someone has to answer questions and write blog posts. You need facilities staff too – someone has to build new tools and services and pages.

5 Libraries need goals, and websites are no different. Preferably, website and social media goals are woven throughout the library's strategic plan. You need to set some goals for usage, growth and engagement, and then try to measure and meet those goals.

6 An awesome library website reaches beyond its webbish boundaries. A library does this by establishing outposts on social media sites. For example, a library can create a Facebook page, and also add a Facebook 'Like' button to its website blog posts.

7 An awesome library website needs to reach into people's pockets and purses . . . via a mobile website. If your customers really value your library and its services, they will put you on their speed-dial, add you to their Facebook friends list, and retweet the events you're holding next week. Create a mobile-friendly website, and your customers can do these things while at home, while standing in a long grocery store line, or during a quick break at work.

Search Engine Optimization (SEO)

A huge part of communication is making sure as many people as possible see your existing messages. Another way to market without significant investment is to improve your online discoverability, through Search Engine

Optimization, known as SEO. In short, this process aims to increase the visibility and ranking of your website in search engines (through organic means, rather than by paying to have your links featured at the top). Marketing is about outreach, and a crucial part of outreach is making sure people can find you on the internet.

SEO is such a buzz-word (or buzz-acronym) among internet consultants and 'marketing experts' that it is easy to treat it with some suspicion. But it *is* really important – particularly when you take into account the behaviour of most internet users. Most search engines display ten results per page, and most users only click on the top two or three – as information professionals we might delve a little deeper than that, but our behaviour isn't typical of our users. A page on the second or third page of Google will get around 1% of the traffic (that is, people actually clicking on their link) that the site ranked first on the first page will get; once you get past page three of the results, chances are hardly anyone will find the link at all.

This is arguably most important in the public library sector (with school, academic and special libraries often having captive audiences), as there is great potential to snare new users, both physical and virtual, by appearing in the results of their online searches. However, because we know that most people start their information searches from a search engine rather than the library's website – 84% of college-age users, for example (OCLC, 2006) – *every* library should be optimizing their websites, for all of the reasons listed above. If redesigning your homepage or creating new social media presences requires a time-commitment you can't afford to make, then SEO is more important than ever in your marketing efforts; it doesn't take a huge amount of time, so it doesn't cost much money.

The basics of SEO

1 People search Google and other search engines with keywords. You need to know what keywords people use to search, and whether or not your website is getting hits for those keywords.
2 You can find out what people are searching for via various free tools. Donna Feddern is an expert on SEO and libraries – she suggests using Wordtracker's Free Keyword Suggestion Tool and the Google Adwords Keyword Tool online (Feddern, 2011a) to type in a keyword. Another option is Google Insights. You are then presented with statistics as to how many searches are being conducted on those keywords, and what

the similar/related keywords or phrases are, with figures for those too. Try it – it's a revealing exercise.

3 You can then ensure your website is a destination for such searches by putting the most popular and important key words in key places: the titles, headings and meta-description on your website, and tags and categories on your blog-posts.

4 Feddern coined the concept of '5 words your library should OWN on Google' (Feddern, 2011b). Her suggestions are aimed at public libraries: 'book club', 'free Wi-Fi', 'volunteer opportunities', 'family events' and 'homework help'. Every library will have different key offerings, so the 5 words you choose to focus on may be different to those listed here; it will vary greatly by sector. The important thing, as ever, is to speak the language of your stakeholders.

A practical example of how SEO can help your library

To contextualize all this, let's work through a specific example. Let's say my public library offers free Wi-Fi, and wants to attract new customers who come in for that (but eventually end up staying and using other resources). I want to make sure my website is getting hits when people are searching for free Wi-Fi in my area, so I go to Google Insights at www.google.com/insights/search/ and compare some search terms. I compared 'free Wi-Fi', 'free internet', and 'free online access' – in the UK, over the last 24 months. The results (when I did this for January 2010–January 2012) are shown in Figure 5.1 on the next page.

Despite what I would have expected, 'free internet' actually scores much more highly than 'free Wi-Fi' – the former is what people are searching for all the time. So, armed with this knowledge, I edit the library web pages so that the information about free Wi-Fi mentions the phrase 'free internet' (in the metatags in particular) and thus my library has been optimized for search engines. Next time people search for 'free internet', my library and its free Wi-Fi will be higher up the list of search results.

Mobile websites

Closely related to the library website is the mobile site, as David indicated in his seventh tip above. This is a bull whose horns we really need to grasp sooner rather than later as an industry – our users will increasingly expect

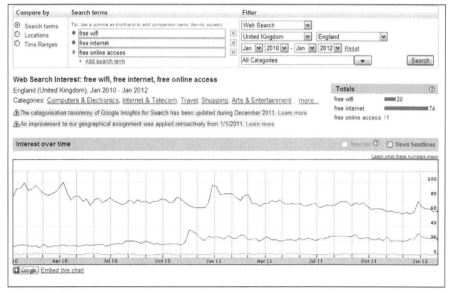

Figure 5.1 *Google Insights example*

library websites and catalogues which they can access from their phones, tablets and other mobile devices. If there is one overriding principle to mobile library websites, it is that 'responsive design' is a must. Responsive design in this context means that when a patron accesses your regular library website or catalogue from their mobile device, it will appear in its mobile-ready form because it 'knows' it is being accessed via mobile. This is as opposed to (a) the regular desktop site appearing on the mobile device or (b) users having to visit a separate URL to access a mobile version.

An additional option is mobile applications, known as apps, which are extremely popular. People use apps for everything from reading newspapers, to watching videos, to planning their schedules. Users download an app and install it on their phone, as opposed to accessing a version of a normal website which is tailored for mobile use. If a library is to develop an app, it needs to be more than just the mobile site with a few added bells and whistles – it needs purpose, function and utility. Jumping onto the app bandwagon is only worth it if the technology is fulfilling an existing need, rather than creating its own, self-fulfilling need. One worthwhile thing to include in a library app is a QR Code scanner; that way, if you decide to market using QR Codes (more on which in Chapter 7) those users utilizing your app will already have the equipment and software they need to engage with them.

The University of Singapore's Aaron Tay provides an expert's view on Web 2.0 in Chapter 7, but for this part of the book I asked him to describe the fundamentals of making a great mobile-ready library website. You can also read Aaron's comparison of 40 mobile websites online (Tay, 2011).

Case study 10: Mobile options for library websites | Aaron Tay

Engaging with users using mobile technology is a broad topic, including use of SMS reference, QR Codes, mobile databases, tablet use, etc. But the basis of every mobile strategy for libraries would still be the mobile library website (including the mobile library catalogue). There are two aspects to this: first deciding what services to offer, secondly making them usable.

Most library mobile sites are surprisingly similar, offering a mobile library catalogue, opening hours, location maps, news, links to social media accounts, etc. However, while such services are expected, usage doesn't seem to be high – at least compared to desktop use.

The experience of University of Amsterdam is typical: they found that the 'killer app' was in fact the ability to view the number of workstations/PCs available and not traditional web services like the library catalogue (Koster, 2010). Boopsie, which is popular with libraries for creating both mobile websites and native apps, announced that non-catalogue services were more popular than the catalogue (PRWeb, 2010).

Given such results for the basic mobile site, I would suggest libraries look for low-cost options. Together with Tiffini Travis, I wrote about low-cost options used by libraries to create mobile sites including Wordpress and LibGuides (Tay and Travis, 2011). Other popular options include LibraryAnywhere and Boopsie, which provide the ability to create native apps for a variety of smartphones, as well as the ability to 'mobilize' the catalogue, which is useful if the library catalogue you are using doesn't already offer a mobile option.

We also offer a couple of mobile heuristics to test with when creating your mobile site. One which is really obvious is that users should be auto-redirected to the mobile version when they visit the library site using a mobile device (i.e. responsive design), though we have found that this doesn't always happen.

For academic libraries, there is an option to work with the university and to include library functions in a unified university mobile site (either mobile web or native app). There has been quite a lot of debate over whether to offer only a mobile web version or to offer native apps, the pros and cons of both are pretty well known, but one advantage of a mobile web version is that it can be easily included in an overall university mobile offering, whether the university offers an overall mobile web or native app. For example, at the National University of Singapore, we have a mobile app of our courseware that is pretty popular, as it includes the ability to watch webcasts of lectures, download lecture documents, sync course timetables with the phone's calendar and so on. We have also benefited by including our mobile catalogue (mobile web version) into the app, which is paying dividends, as this has become our top referrer (the link by which most users arrive at the catalogue).

The other major area in mobile for academic libraries is the handling of mobile databases. At this stage it is really unclear if users really want to access journal articles and e-books on mobile phones, surveys having been mixed; some have users saying they seldom do so, but indicate they might be interested if mobile sites are offered. Libraries generally rely on the vendors to provide mobile options for databases and increasingly they have begun doing so, including mobile versions for EBSCOhost, JSTOR, Cambridge Journal online, Web of Science, Scopus, etc. Most currently offer mobile web versions but some, like EBSCO and Elsevier, offer native apps. Authentication methods for native apps are currently non-standardized, so it might be a good idea for libraries to maintain a guide or page on such resources.

In terms of actually marketing the mobile version of a library website, it's hard to beat the University of Michigan's just-the-right-side-of-cheeky campaign created by Liene Karels (concept) and Suzanne Chapman (design and execution), an example of which is shown in Figure 5.2.

A final word on websites: when attempting to measure which marketing channels are having the most impact with your target audience, custom URLs are really useful. URL redirection services like Bit.ly (www.bit.ly) are primarily used for shortening web-links, making them easier to share on social media – for example, I used Bit.ly to shorten **www.librarymarketingtoolkit.com** to **http://bit.ly/uH2V94**.

Where this becomes particularly relevant to marketing and evaluation is in the fact that you can create multiple Bit.ly addresses for the same web page – for instance, for the library homepage – using multiple Bit.ly accounts. This means that, to take a basic example, you could tweet one version of the URL, put another on a flyer and put a third on the free pencils you give out at reception – and then check the statistics on your Bit.ly accounts showing the number of clicks each has had, and see which

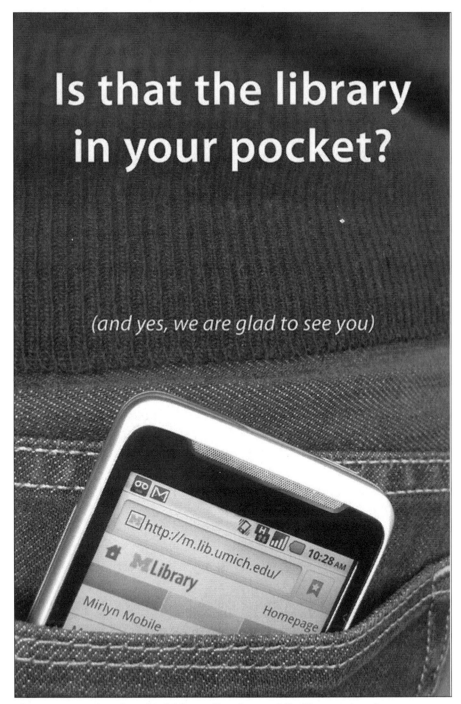

Figure 5.2 *University of Michigan Libraries' mobile library advertisement*

promotional device is driving the most web traffic to the library homepage.

Another utility of the Bit.ly account is the ability to create custom URLs; having created my shortening of the Library Marketing Toolkit web address above, I was then able to customize it to http://bit.ly/librarymarketing – if you put that into a web browser, you'll be redirected to the home page. This is really handy when the URL you want people to remember isn't simply www.nameofyourlibrary.org but a more complicated link with a more complicated address. Claim your custom URLs quickly though, because once someone applies a custom URL to a website it will belong to that particular site forever . . .

E-mail

Marketing with e-mail is usually free, but it's a tricky area. When done well, there's no better way to speak directly to a target audience. When done badly, it can alienate the very people you're trying to attract, as they resent seeing yet another e-mail pop into their inbox which isn't directed specifically at them.

Promotion via e-mail is particularly good if you want people to take the action of visiting part of your library website or catalogue; the immediacy of being able to click on a link in an e-mail and see a website right then and there is a very powerful tool. People simply do not go back and check a website later if they write down the URL after a presentation, or read it on paper. They need the minimum barrier between themselves and the goal of viewing the website to assess it – in the e-mail's case, just one click of the mouse. Catch people with a good e-mail, and this can be a form of marketing that yields instant results.

For special libraries and academic libraries, there may be circumstances in which it is possible to e-mail each recipient individually rather than sending a mass e-mail to an entire department. Clearly this will take much longer – e-mailing 25 people individually will always eat up more of your day then e-mailing them all at once, even if the e-mail is exactly the same each time – but it's worth considering whether the gains are in fact worth the extra time. Busy people are more inclined to delete an e-mail after only skim-reading it, or even not reading it at all, if they think it is a generic communication rather than something aimed specifically at them.

What are the tricks to turning people on rather than switching them off? Alison Wallbutton provides the final case study of this chapter to give some expert advice. Alison is the Business Librarian at Massey University, New Zealand, and writes and presents on the subject of marketing libraries.

Case study 11: How to market with e-mail | Alison Wallbutton

Is there anybody who doesn't feel that they are drowning in e-mail already? So why might e-mail be useful as a marketing channel for our customers? It does have its advantages – it's a quick way of distributing your communications; it's easy for recipients to share your messages with others; it's environmentally friendly (although some customers may feel you are just trying to get on the green bandwagon unless it is part of a bigger green strategy!).

As far as disadvantages go – yes, there is the e-mail overload factor. And you also have to bear in mind that it is unlikely to be a communication channel used by young people. I recall hearing teenagers participating at Stephen Abram's session at the 2006 LIANZA (Library and Information Association of New Zealand Aotearoa) conference, talking about how e-mail was something they used for communicating with their grandparents . . .

So here are some tips to consider:

1 Have a think about what works for you and for others. Do some informal surveying with your customers, friends, colleagues. What works for you as a consumer? I have managed to sign up to e-mails from various retail stores and other companies – some end up being more useful for me than others. Previews, discount vouchers and special offers are always welcome! Would these appeal to your customers? You might include occasional freebies such as vouchers for free DVD hire, or free printing – especially for those who are signing up to your e-mails for the first time.

2 You can also use e-mails to encourage your customers to check out your other marketing channels – like Facebook or Twitter, and provide incentives for them to do so.

3 Take care with the way you write your e-mails. You need to convey an interesting message that gets over the 'so what?' factor. People will need a reason to read your e-mail! Make your e-mail heading punchy and interesting, but be careful not to let it be read as spam. If you are reworking a promotional message used in another channel (say a blog entry or a poster), take the key points and rewrite them to grab attention. Keep really

important information at the top of the e-mail – don't make people read all the way down for the good stuff.

4 Think about the look of your e-mails too – be sure to incorporate your branding. At Massey University Library http://library.massey.ac.nz we select relevant items from our library blog and e-mail them as news headlines to our academics, using a branded e-mail template. This allows us to spread our messages using a different communication channel and to reuse content that has already been written.

5 Be careful with how often you send out e-mail communications. Do your customers really want a regular newsletter that they have to deal with, or would they rather be delighted with an occasional gem?

For more information and further reading, go to this chapter's web page at **www.librarymarketingtoolkit.com/p/introduction-to-online-marketing.html**. Once the fundamental web presence is working successfully, the library can then start communicating directly with its users via social media; that's what the next chapter is all about.

CHAPTER 6
Marketing with social media

The term 'social media' describes any kind of online platform in which the users can exchange content. That content can be actual digital objects (films, music and other files) or just opinions, news and views. As such, these platforms represent a fabulous possibility for libraries. It is not something to fret about or agonize over; it is an opportunity to be seized. Via social media libraries can market directly to their users and potential users, and engage them in the kind of proper *dialogue* which marketing should be all about.

Using social media as a marketing channel is very straightforward. Here is a quick analogy to try and explain the value of social media to the sceptics. Imagine you have a poster advertising your library – it contains some (static) information, presents it well, and you put your poster up all over town and hope the right people see it. You never know for sure how many people see it, or what they think of it. But you cross your fingers and hope it works. Now imagine a poster which is interactive and whose information can change from day to day – imagine taking that poster individually to hundreds or even thousands of potential users at once and getting their feedback on it, answering their questions, even monitoring what they say about the poster in your absence and adapting it to suit them better. That's what social media does.

And on top of all that, it's mostly free.

Do your patrons use social media?

The short answer is: yes. The longer answer is: of course, there will be exceptions, but increasingly more and more of your target audience will be using one form of social media or another. Worldwide, people spend on average more time on social media each week than they do on e-mail (TNS, 2010).

At the time of writing there are 11.7 million active social networkers in Canada, 114.5 million in the USA and 7 million in Australia. The UK has 19.3

million active social networkers (GlobalWebIndex, 2011) – when you consider how many of the approximately 65 million people in the UK are either too young or too old, that represents a huge percentage of the population. Throughout this chapter the figures can only go so far to represent the situation, as they are changing all the time – in most cases, increasing rapidly. By the time you read this, the numbers above will almost certainly have increased considerably.

The rest of this chapter assumes some familiarity with social media platforms. To list all the different types of social media tools and what they do would leave very little space for tips on how to market with them; for this reason I've put a basic overview of social media platforms in the Appendix. If you've never used social media before, it might be best to read the Appendix first – it begins on page 197 – and them come back and finish off this chapter.

The tools we'll be discussing in this chapter are blogs, microblogs, and social networks. Other Web 2.0 tools and new technologies, such as wikis, QR Codes, video sharing and so on, are discussed separately in the next chapter.

The case studies in this chapter are from the British Library on all aspects of their social media marketing, Manchester Libraries on their use of Facebook, and New York Public Library on their use of Twitter.

General principles of marketing with social media

Know why you're there

Each of your library's social media profiles should have a purpose and a focus of its own.

Don't over-commit

Defunct social media profiles can do more harm than good – so make sure you can provide enough resources to run each profile well, or don't run it at all.

Get the tone right

Because Web 2.0 is all about dialogue, the tone you use on social media sites should be conversational. Many libraries start off rather stiffly on social networks – that's okay, as long as over time you become less formal and relax a little. What you should be aiming for is informal but not overly familiar, friendly but not overly personal, colloquial but grammatically, syntactically and orthographically correct. It's a hard balance to strike! But if you're friendly, informal, authoritative and you spell everything correctly, you're more than halfway there.

Listen!

Marketing is an ongoing conversation between the marketer and the target audience, so social media platforms are a fantastic way to listen to what is being said by that audience. Imagine how many focus groups you'd have to set up to garner as much feedback as you can from asking questions to hundreds of followers via social media. Many marketers talk about 'the one in four rule' on social media platforms, and on Twitter in particular – only one in four updates or tweets should be directly promoting your own brand, and the other three should be replies; reconstituting other people's content; or something else not directly related to whatever it is you are trying to market. I wouldn't advise sticking rigidly to this but it does give some indication of just how important the 'conversation versus broadcast' principle is.

Get the message across

In my opinion, library use of Web 2.0 platforms should be aiming to accomplish the following: add value in order to increase engagement so that you can deliver key messages to a wider audience. In other words, make your Twitter feed (or whatever) more interesting so that more people follow you, so that more people then get the really important messages you want to market about your library. The added-value parts (the replies, the links to external content and so on) are what give your social media presences personality, and the personality is what draws in more followers. Then when you have the really important messages to impart (new opening hours, new collections, new services or whatever you really need to convey) there are more members of your captive audience. If on the other hand you *only* communicate those really important messages, people will think you're boring and so you'll reach fewer users and potential users.

Make social media part of something bigger

Your social media marketing shouldn't exist in isolation – it works best when combined with more traditional promotion. More on this below.

Act quickly if it all goes wrong

Sometimes human error creeps in and the person tweeting or updating a Facebook status gets mixed up between their personal and institutional accounts. Inappropriate content (most usually simple opinions or anecdotes) can be inadvertently shared via social media and when this happens, respond quickly, honestly, and apologize with the appropriate level of seriousness. A little slip does not require a huge and sombre apology – that only draws attention to what has happened and makes people overestimate its gravity. A quick 'Oops, sorry – wrong account there!' may well be fine. On the other side of the coin, a serious slip (such as Tweeting something obscene or otherwise offensive) needs swift and decisive action. An hour is an absolute eternity in social media terms – the mishap may have been retweeted by others a hundred times by the time you delete the original offending item . . .

Hit the ground running

Remember that the basis of many initial followings on social media is reciprocity. User X follows or 'friends' User Y, and User Y gets a message or e-mail telling them so. Out of curiosity they check out User X's profile, and decide to follow them back if they're interesting. For this reason, following people is a great way to get those initial followers yourself, and good quality content is essential right from the start, even before you fully launch your social media profile into the public sphere. When you do launch, do so in a big way – don't just promote your new accounts via the website, but within the walls of the library too. Companies like Moo.com do brightly coloured and attractive double-sided business cards in all kinds of designs – why not have some made with your library's name on one side and your social media URLs on the other? These can be placed strategically around the library, and distributed at relevant events. Other ways of enabling people to discover your social media presences right away are to add a link to e-mail signatures of library staff, and of course getting library champions to spread the word to their contacts.

Utilize social proof

Finally, no one wants to be first onto an empty dance floor – it's worth having a few followers from the off to convince others to join in. Before promoting a Facebook or Twitter account, it's worth connecting with as many other accounts as possible so that there's something to show people – so follow your library with your own personal account, and perhaps ask other library staff and a few friends or associates to do the same. This leads to 'social proof' – the phenomenon whereby people copy the actions of others because they assume those others must know what they are doing. Andreas Pouros (2011) gives some good examples of social proof on the eConsultancy website: buskers 'seeding' their tips jar to encourage people to donate, and canned laughter on TV comedies leading the audience to perceive a show as funnier than the same show without the canned laughter, being two of them. He also describes a famous experiment in which a man stared at the sky: he was largely ignored. Then four others were hired to stare at the sky too – so many passers-by stopped to join in, convinced that there must be *something* to see, that the whole thing had to be abandoned due to stopping local traffic. In other words, there's no easier way to convince people to follow your library on social media platforms than for them to see other people already doing so; thereafter your success self-perpetuates. This isn't to say having huge numbers of followers is an end in itself, of course; it is very much a means to an end, that end being the ability to engage in dialogue with relevant users and potential users.

Before we go into the specific marketing applications of each tool, we can get a feel for how libraries can market with social media via a case study, from the British Library.

Case study 12: Social media at the British Library's Business and IP Centre | Frances Taylor

The British Library's Business and IP Centre is a multifaceted organization – it is attached to a public library but its operation has more in common with a Special Library. They use five main social media platforms for a variety of purposes: two networks, blogs, microblogs and video sharing. Marketing Manager Frances Taylor gives an in-depth overview of their marketing activity.

First, can you tell us which social media platforms you use, and what you use them for?

We use all the big social media sites: Facebook, Twitter, LinkedIn and YouTube. Our aim is to raise awareness of the Business and IP Centre and promote our services, to provide a platform for entrepreneurs to network and to engage with our partners and customers.

Social media has been invaluable in helping us to engage with our target audience of entrepreneurs and small businesses. We have found that each site works well in different ways:

Facebook is great for promoting events and running competitions. However, it isn't as business-focused and doesn't work as well as a platform for serious debate.

Twitter allows us to stay in touch with our partner organizations and stakeholders more easily. We use it to monitor our brand and as a customer services tool. If a customer has a negative or positive experience at the British Library and writes about it on Twitter, our aim is to pick it up quickly and to respond.

LinkedIn is useful for giving people a place to engage with each other. It works well for business discussions and promoting events. Although it can be difficult trying to stop users of our LinkedIn group from adding spam.

We run a series of high-profile events called 'Inspiring Entrepreneurs', with previous speakers including Lord Sugar, Stelios Haji-Ioannou and the late Dame Anita Roddick. We film all of our events and put them on our YouTube channel. So far we have had over 218,000 video plays.

Lastly, the manager of the Centre, Neil Infield, and our expert in patents, Steve van Dulken, both write blogs for the Centre. They get thousands of views every month and drive the third most traffic to our website after search engines and Facebook. We have found that blogs can be a useful way of enhancing your ranking on Google.

The process of marketing is about understanding the market as well as promoting services to that market – do you use social media to gather information on users, potential users, business partners and other organizations in your area?

Definitely! Our approach to social media is to make sure that we spend as much time following and listening to other people as posting information about ourselves. We try to immerse ourselves in the world of business support and stay informed of all the latest news and trends.

When organizations only post information about themselves on Twitter it can be very off-putting. I use the analogy of going to a party – you wouldn't stand in a corner of the room and shout at people. It's exactly the same on Twitter. You need to ensure that you're interested in the people that you follow, and that you engage with them.

Can you tell us about any interesting social media campaigns you have run?
We are particularly proud of a campaign we ran for an 'Inspiring Entrepreneurs' event on social media. We arranged for the event to be streamed live over the internet and online viewers could submit questions to the panel of speakers. We encouraged viewers on-site and online to use our Twitter hashtag #bipcsocial. We also partnered with our equivalent in the USA, the New York Public Library. They put on a free event where their members could watch the event live from one of their meeting rooms. On top of this, Real Business magazine and Business Zone wrote live blogs about the event. Lastly, to bring it all together, we ran a live Twitter feed on the stage which, admittedly, was quite daunting for the speakers, but great fun.

I'm really interested in the relationship between social media and physical spaces, as I think the two can work extremely well together. Last year we ran a networking event called 'Facebook vs. LinkedIn' where we invited our followers from each of the sites to come together and meet face-to-face. It was a big success, and places sold out in a few hours.

More recently, I have been experimenting with competitions and using Twitter hashtags to generate user content.

Was there resistance to using social media initially? Did you get comments along the lines of 'I'm not sure our users really want to be friends with us on a social network'?
Luckily, staff at the British Library are open-minded towards social media and I didn't face any resistance. I have also been an active user of social media in my personal life for a number of years, which I think really helped when persuading other people of its value.

Saying that, it's important to approach it from a business perspective. When persuading your managers to let you have a presence, you need to be really clear of the outcomes that you want, how you will ensure quality and how you will monitor success. One of the big challenges is time – social media can take a lot of resource to set up and maintain. Saying that, in this economic climate social media is also an attractive marketing tool to use, in that it is often free.

Can you explain a little about how using social media fits in with the rest of your more traditional marketing efforts?

I'm trained as a traditional marketer, therefore I see social media as one piece of a larger puzzle. Often I will run campaigns that involve the full marketing mix, including press, e-newsletters and e-flyers, the website, advertising campaigns, working with partners, etc. By using a range of media, you can ensure that your campaigns have maximum impact.

In an ideal world, an entrepreneur would see an advert for the Centre, read an article about us in a newspaper, be recommended to us by a partner organization and then follow us on Twitter.

It's also important to ensure that people can find you easily on social media sites. You can add links from your e-mails and website as a way of gaining more followers.

What advice would you give to a library just starting to promote their services using social media?
Here are my top five tips for libraries:

1 Have a strategy. Be very clear about who your target audience is, which social media sites your customers use and why you're doing it.
2 Start small. It's better to do one thing properly than to end up with lots of sad, neglected profiles all over the web.
3 Think about success measures. It isn't about having 1000 followers on Twitter: what happened as a result of them following you? Did you change their behaviour or their perception of your library?
4 Develop a tone of voice. You need to think about your writing style – ours is informal but we are careful to ensure that we use correct grammar and spelling. It's useful to have a 'house style'.
5 Train your staff and share ideas: I like the idea of developing a culture within organizations that allows people to experiment and support one another. It's important to ensure that any social media activity is of the highest quality, but you also give staff the opportunity to experiment. A common mistake is when organizations say that they want to 'control' social media and set up complicated sign-off processes for messages. For me, it is all about developing people's skills and confidence.

With these general principles in mind, let's look at specific platforms, with some case studies to expand upon the most important. One of the absolutely key things Frances Taylor says in the British Library case study above is 'It's better to do one thing properly than to end up with lots of sad, neglected profiles all over the web.' I can't stress how much I agree with this – social media marketing is remarkably un-intensive in terms of time versus reward, but *it is a commitment*. Only create a social media profile in your library's name if there are plans in place to maintain it – not just for six months or even a year, but for as long as your users are on that platform. For this reason, I'd recommend developing your social media profiles in roughly the order below.

Twitter

Many more people are on the social network Facebook than are on the microblogging platform Twitter (www.twitter.com) – around five times as many at the time of writing – but there are a few reasons I'd advise starting out with the latter. First, it takes very little work to set up a Twitter profile, less than any other platform. Secondly, research has shown that users engage with libraries more on Twitter than on other networks; they seem to prefer interacting via this medium. And thirdly, Twitter users are much more influential than those on other networks, so can help build your brand. A report from Exact Target (2011) found that regular Twitter users are generally more active and participatory on the web: they blog, they comment on other blogs, they review things online and so on. They are, in fact, three times more likely to amplify (draw attention to) a brand than a regular Facebook user. This makes them a great asset to have – word of mouth is, after all, a hugely powerful marketing tool, as we have already discussed. As Sherilynn Macale of thenextweb.com puts it, 'in essence: what happens on Twitter, doesn't stay on Twitter' (Macale, 2011).

Getting started

So you've registered for a Twitter account for your library – what next?

1 Firstly choose as short a username as you can whilst still making sense to people – famously Twitter only allows people 140 characters per tweet, so users dislike having to sacrifice too many of those to the name of the person or institution they're talking to.
2 Put in a bio. Don't do anything else until you've updated the bio – and try and convey why people might enjoy engaging with you, rather than just putting in factual information. Instead of just writing 'This is the

Twitter account for the Library of X' you could put 'Library of X, tweeting useful tips for using our resources, recommended reads, details of our workshops and more besides. Got a question? Send us a tweet!'

3 Upload a profile picture right away – people on Twitter are hugely put off by the default avatar. Although Twitter is a personal medium, a profile picture of a library is inevitably going to be of a building rather than an individual, which is fine. Keep in mind that most people will be viewing the picture very small on screen, so an arty shot of your library taken from far away won't look great in everyday use.

4 Upload a background image for your profile. When people click on your name or go to your Twitter URL, they'll see your most recent tweets, your profile picture, your bio, and some information about who you follow. All this appears floating atop the background of your choice, and now is the time to show off a really nice picture of your library. If you want to make your account more personal, upload a background image which includes photos and nameplates for the people who tweet via the library account. You could even combine this with a technique the delivery service UPS use – they edit their profile each time someone new takes over tweeting duties, to say 'On duty: [employee's first name]'. This kind of thing helps ease the transition of the institutional account into the personal realm that is social media.

Start tweeting, then start following

5 You now have everything in place to start actually tweeting. Over a period of a couple of hours, write about ten tweets. Most people's Twitter accounts start off with the usual sort of 'Hello world!' introductory tweet – that's fine, although tweets along the lines of 'Thought we'd find out what this Twitter lark was all about' are to be avoided. If possible start strong – 'Hi all! This is Library of X. We're on Twitter to share information, news, advice and links with users and non-users alike.' Then get stuck in to doing exactly that with a mixed approach – tweet useful links to useful resources on your own site, ask a question ('What kind of thing would you like to see us tweeting about on here?' often elicits really useful responses) and perhaps retweet (or RT) some content from another account, which your potential followers might find relevant (e.g. 'Do these match your top 10? RT @SomeAccount Readers choose top 10 books this decade.') The point of these first ten tweets is to provide a

microcosm of the kind of content you intend to provide via Twitter, so that when people click on your profile (which they are going to do after step 6) they'll be greeted with something which inspires them to follow you.

6 Now, and only now, should you start to follow other people and institutions. When a Twitter account gains a new follower, its administrator will receive an e-mail telling them of the fact, and giving them some information about that new follower (unless they've turned this feature off). Most Twitter users will at least give the new follower a cursory glance and decide whether or not to follow them back. This decision usually depends on the profile (picture and bio particularly) and the user's last few tweets – this is why it's essential to undertake steps 1–5 and have everything sorted before starting to follow other people.

For an institutional account it's good to follow several institutions which regularly feature retweetable content. By which I mean information which is nothing to do with your library specifically, but which may nevertheless be of value or interest to your users if you RT it to them. These include the Twitter accounts of major newspapers and news organizations, and local institutions. For public libraries, following other council services is a must; for academic libraries, following other departments within the university (not forgetting student-run enterprises like the student newspaper) is also essential. The idea is that your followers will come to appreciate that you will keep them in the loop with important events, as well as just library-related matters. It adds value to your account.

Another category of accounts to follow is that of 'exemplars' – essentially, other library and archive Twitter accounts who successfully engage with and market to many followers, so you can pick up some tips for best practice from watching them operate. The final and most important category is 'Users and Potential Users'. This is also the most tricky. When people follow you, it is often possible to ascertain whether they fit into this category by checking their bio and location, but proactively seeking out users is more difficult. One good way is to use searches to find out who is talking about your library – there's more information on how to do that below.

I would recommend you sort these groups of people and institutions into lists on Twitter, making it easier to find the content you're looking for. Once you start following more than a couple of hundred people, it becomes tricky to scan through and find the kind of content to which you might wish to draw your followers' attention; having a 'local institutions' list saved on Twitter becomes a useful shortcut, particularly if you don't have much time to tweet on a given day.

Taking an established library Twitter account to the next level

Most libraries feel their way gently into using Twitter. Early tweets are characterized by a stiffness and formality which doesn't quite suit social media, but this is understandable because it feels odd for an institutional account to rush straight in to being colloquial and personable. The important thing is to become friendlier over time.

The 'Twitter as party' analogy used by Frances Taylor above can be extended. Not only do people at parties want to be asked questions rather than just listen to you go on about yourself for hours, but people at parties begin to give more of themselves as they settle in to the social situation. They become more friendly and more confident – as should you with your library Twitter account over time.

You can begin to ask your followers questions and RT their answers; recommendations are always good for this, books being the obvious candidate, but there are plenty of other interesting topics such as films, music, museums, even online tools. Services like Twtpoll (http://twtpoll.com) enable you to poll your followers quickly and easily, and provide graphs of the results for you to tweet or display in a blog post. There are also specific things you can do to operate in a more advanced way – for example, setting up some Twitter searches.

Anyone (even non-Twitter users) can go to https://twitter.com/#!/search-advanced and set up an advanced search; if you have a Twitter account you can save that search so that it's quickly available on an ongoing basis.

The first and most obvious search to set up is one on the name of your library. This way you'll know what people are saying about you even if they aren't using your Twitter username in their tweets. At my own institution, the University of York, we have searches set up on the names of our major library sites, e.g. 'JB Morrell Library'. The next searches to set up are colloquial derivatives of your library's name: for example a search on 'York Uni Library'.

Then set up a locational search. A locational search will pick up any tweets sent from a specific geographical area – it is worth noting that this only picks up tweets from users who have enabled 'geo-tagging' in their profile settings, and who are tweeting from mobile devices. The majority of users will have geo-tagging turned off, so this search will likely not yield as many results as the previous ones we have described. It is still worth setting up, however, because when you can help a user who would otherwise not have known the library was on Twitter at all, it is extremely satisfying and represents very good marketing. On the advanced search screen there is a 'Places' field – when you type something into this box a sub-field appears below it entitled 'Within this distance'. At York we have a locational search on the word 'library' within one mile of our postcode to pick up tweets from students to their peers like 'In the library: anyone know where the sociology books are now?' We put the local public library's name into the 'None of these words' field to ensure that we don't pick up tweets pertaining to that institution.

Depending on the nature of your library (and on how much time you want to devote to this), you may want to set up other locational searches on keywords which fit your demographic, for example on 'research', 'cite', 'journal' or even 'information'. For more on 'social monitoring' see Andy Burkhardt's case study on the website, at **www.librarymarketingtoolkit.com/p/advanced-twitter-search-for-social.html**.

The final tip for taking your Twitter marketing to the next level is to use some tools to analyse your Twitter use. There are a million and one out there, so the important thing is to stick to the ones which will provide you with *actionable results*. Which is to say, once you learn what the tool has to tell you, can you use that information actually to change something? Just knowing that you picked up eight new followers last week and were RT'd ten times, does not, in itself, provide useful material for strategic marketing. But there are tools which do:

1   Use Twocation to find out where your followers are based. Significant overseas followers might vary the times you tweet information. This is particularly relevant in the Special Libraries environment. www.twocation.com

2   Use Tweetstats to find out what percentage of your tweets are @ replies or RTs. This gives you an idea of how interactive your account really is. If less than 25% of your tweets involve other people, then make a conscious decision to increase engagement with your followers. Record the percentage over time and make sure it rises. http://tweetstats.com

3   Use Klout to find out your influence. Don't get caught up with your overall score – Klout uses an algorithm to rate your overall influence, which prizes number-of-followers for number-of-followers' sake, which is

not something I'd agree with and it certainly doesn't work for libraries. However, there are sub-scores within your overall Klout score, and these are interesting. Use Klout to track your 'Network Influence' and 'Amplification Probability' – these are much more useful scores to measure and record because they show how likely your followers are to act on what you tweet. An engaged follower tends to be an active follower, so again you should be attempting to engineer a rise in your score for these two categories. http://klout.com

As more and more libraries embrace Twitter, one library is always held up as the most successful example of using the medium well: New York Public Library (@NYPL). It is to them that we turn for the final word on Twitter in this chapter.

Case study 13: Twitter at NYPL | Kathy Saeed

NYPL does social media in a BIG way. Their 'Connect with NYPL' page (www.nypl.org/voices/connect-nypl) lists ten different platforms at the time of writing, including the usual suspects Facebook, YouTube and Flickr, but with some more advanced outlets like iTunes and Foursquare. Because the individual neighbourhood libraries also have their own social media outputs, there are in fact more than 100 accounts under the NYPL banner. The Library's overall social media efforts are spearheaded by the Marketing and Communications department. On the flagship level, NYPL has implemented a unique decentralized staffing model consisting of over ten editors from different departments of the Library. NYPL also offers its staff writing, blogging and social media training for those looking to get involved with social media on a local level.

There's very little point in recording figures for social media use in a book like this, because of course the figures change all the time – in NYPL's case, they will undoubtedly have increased a lot by the time the reader sees this. But suffice to say the numbers are huge – only the Library of Congress appears to attract more followers across various platforms, and I'd speculate that a higher percentage of those are librarians than is the case with NYPL's accounts. As a marketing tool, social media has most value when it is outward facing, towards users and potential users – although, of course, there is marketing value in improving your reputation within the field too. NYPL seems to manage both.

Their Twitter presence @NPYL (www.twitter.com/nypl) has well over 100,000 followers and won the library a NonProfit PR Award in 2010 (see

www.prnewsonline.com/pr_awards/nonprofit/14336.html). On a given day, ten or more NYPL staff will be contributing to its flagship Twitter account. They use tools like Hootsuite (an application through which to use Twitter, available at www.hootsuite.com) to co-ordinate their messaging, and SocialFlow (www.socialflow.com) for automated tweeting of blog content. Kathy Saeed, Marketing Associate at the library, took me through their operation.

Tell us how you approach the issue of multiple contributors to your main account. I understand you use scheduled tweets, and also assign tweets and responses to specific members of staff?

In order to successfully operate a Twitter feed with multiple contributors, communication is key. With Hootsuite, designated staff members are able to plan and schedule messages on a regular basis. Before tweeting on behalf of @NYPL all team members are given a thorough walkthrough of the tools used, they learn what other team members are working on, and what makes for an interesting tweet. Every day staff from our Collections team will tweet a quote from a book and link to the Library's BiblioCommons catalogue. We also have staff tweeting our Spanish materials as it is the second most spoken language amongst our users. Other content includes news, service updates, programs, databases, funs facts, Foursquare tips, as well as automated tweeting of our blog posts through a tool called SocialFlow. The Marketing department maintains an editorial calendar into which additional social media messaging can be plugged for posting to flagship accounts.

Do you have a formal social media strategy as such, or loose guidelines within which all contributors work?

The New York Public Library has developed a formal social media policy as well as training for those interested in doing so on behalf of the institution. Before any branch or division of the Library begins a page or account, the staff member is required to read and review this policy with their supervisor, and to attend training as needed. Loose guidelines are also put into place on a flagship level to make sure we are actively engaging with users on a daily basis.

How do you manage the blend between tweets relating directly to the Library, and more general things?

Our Marketing and Communications team which manages the Library's main Twitter stream takes the time each day to survey the Twitterverse looking for trending topics, current events, and popular content (literary and/or otherwise).

We also look to our fellow cultural institutions, libraries and supporters for interesting and helpful information that might be worth retweeting or repurposing on our other streams. As for Library-related messaging, our decentralized staffing model allows us to provide a little bit of everything to our followers.

With so many followers, I imagine answering all @ replies is pretty much impossible – do you have to prioritize enquiries and if so, how?

We have staff from the Library's Ask NYPL reference service checking in on Twitter every day to address any user inquires. With tools like Hootsuite, our team members are also able to assign different tweets (or inquiries) to the appropriate staff member for assistance. We try and make sure that any questions tweeted directly @NYPL are answered within a few hours.

Apart from NYPL's status as a venerable institution, to what do you attribute the runaway success of the Twitter account?

The runaway success of @NYPL's Twitter account can be largely attributed to the content and resources our staff offers the public through this channel. Consistently providing patrons with service updates, and (for the most part) free and low-cost ways to take advantage of the Library has users coming back for more.

Have you attempted any analysis on the impact your Twitter account (or your social media presence generally) has had on library use?

The Library is using a variety of tools to regularly monitor and report on its various social media accounts and online activity. We are currently using Google Analytics, Convio, Radian6, SocialFlow, Hootsuite and Facebook Insights. As new tools continue to be developed, we are always looking for and testing for more robust reporting methods. Our goal is to continue growing NYPL's audiences on social media, e-communications and driving more web-traffic which we hope will lead to more visits to the Library. In the past, our advocacy campaigns on Twitter have successfully generated letters written to City Council members as well as donations. As of yet, we have not found a way to measure the direct correlation between tweeting and physical library visits.

On a related note, has your recent partnership with Foursquare yielded any results in terms of encouraging library use?

NYPL's partnership with Foursquare helped get the Library on the map in a great way. As the first public library with a Foursquare badge, the partnership generated thousands of brand mentions amongst online users. The badge celebrating the Centennial of NYPL's landmark Stephen A. Schwarzman Building on Fifth Avenue and 42nd Street in New York was unlocked by more than 12,000 users, and tens of thousands are now following NYPL on Foursquare. [There is more information on Foursquare in the next chapter.]

What are the five most important things you'd recommend to other libraries in terms of running a Twitter account that patrons and potential patrons will want to engage with?

1 Tweeting things that are of value to your customers gives them a reason to follow you.
2 Tap into your staff's expert knowledge to share informative and resourceful content with users.
3 Stay active, respond to patron inquires, and plan ahead using an editorial calendar.
4 Don't be afraid to try new things and learn what works best with your audience.
5 Stay relevant and current, but most importantly don't forget to be personable and have a little fun.

Facebook

The social media landscape shifts so quickly that the majority of academic studies on Facebook (www.facebook.com) and libraries are completely out of date because they herald from 2009 or before. There was a time when libraries weren't particularly welcomed by users on Facebook; this is no longer the case. This is not the same world into which a thousand ill-advised library MySpace accounts were born.

Your users are on Facebook. The site has close to a billion active users (perhaps more by the time you read this), and if you think about how many of the world's population don't have access to the internet at all, a billion users equates to a staggering percentage of the people online. Moreover, over 50% of them log in daily (for up-to-date statistics, see www.facebook.com/press/info.php?statistics) meaning there is an opportunity to market to them on an ongoing basis. The final statistic of note is that each user is, on average, connected with 130 other users. So if libraries are producing the kind of high-quality content that gets users to hit the 'like' button, the chances are that lots of new people are going to see the content appearing in their own profiles – amplifying the reach of the library.

Studies have shown (and your own experiences as a user may well confirm this) that people use Facebook differently from any other platform. They open it up in one tab of their internet browser – and then they just leave it open. All day. It is a constant companion to whatever other leisure or work-related activities they undertake on their computers. As such it can help us at pretty much all stages of the marketing lifecycle. You don't have to deliver all the key messages at once, because the opportunity is there to be in contact with users over a long period of time. We can feed into their own daily lifecycle.

A particularly useful role a library Facebook site can have is to 'rescue' useful items which have appeared on the main library website in the past but which could do with re-exposure now. Services or classes or even collections which launched amid much fanfare on your library's website may now be forgotten about by most users and not even seen originally by the rest – use Facebook to draw your users' attention back to things they'd value.

If time is limited, it's straightforward to populate your Facebook page with content from elsewhere in the library. RSS feeds from a library blog, tweets from your Twitter feed, perhaps your library events calendar – all of these can be embedded on the Facebook page so that they automatically update the pages with relevant content.

Two final tips: keep in mind that you can embed a search-box on your Facebook page – to the library OPAC or even to resources like the arts and humanities database JSTOR. And lastly, take advantage of Insights, Facebook's built-in analytics tool; it's powerful and very useful. Use it to learn more about your users, and adapt the content of your pages accordingly – for example, if a high percentage of visitors to your pages are under 25, you can orient the content to suit that demographic.

Case study 14: Facebook at Manchester Libraries | Sue Lawson

Manchester Libraries' (UK) use of Facebook is often cited as being absolutely on the money, and their well designed site has been praised in the influential 'Social Media Examiner' webzine as being one of the best of its kind. They reach over 3,000 people through Facebook – and unlike New York Public Library which enjoys the kind of cult status that would lead people who've never even been to New York to follow them on Twitter, Manchester Libraries' Facebook followers are probably ALL users or potential users – apart from the other library services who follow Manchester to learn from their example. Sue Lawson, who oversees their social media efforts as Service Development Co-ordinator described what works for them.

How do you use Facebook to market the libraries?

Facebook is a shop window for your library service. We update daily with news and links about events, workshops, Wi-Fi, festivals, new books and resources, important messages and changes to services. Facebook makes it easy to include links to specific collections like our archives and photo galleries on Flickr or a time-lapse video of the Manchester Central Library transformation and refurbishment. You can include photos and videos on your page, too; we do this a lot and we also provide quick links to useful web resources that often get buried on the corporate website, making navigation simpler and faster. Staff and council colleagues use the page as a handy way to quickly look up what's on.

Although we indulge in a fair amount of self-promotion, it's not all we do. Too much will just turn off your hard-won fans – they'll get bored and people will start to 'unfollow' you. I make time to find, create and post content that isn't directly related to the library; useful links, Manchester stories, tips, football, bookish furniture, new web service, helpful guides, topical articles, e-book news or exciting updates from other Manchester organizations.

Engaging content is key. A page shouldn't just be a series of broadcasts or announcements. What's the point of a social network if no one is talking? Use your content to get people talking – to the library and to each other. I use Google Alerts and Twitter to find relevant stories and subscribe to lots of blogs in Google Reader and scan the headlines for potential Facebook content. Create a content calendar – you'll find loads of guides online – and use it to organize your content strategy and show your bosses how well you're doing. At the end of each month go through and track how many views and interactions your posts received. This is a good way to see which types of posts are the most popular.

The real beauty of Facebook lies in the connections between people and the potential for your one update to be seen and shared by hundreds and possibly thousands of people. If someone using Facebook finds your update interesting, they can 'like' it or 'share' it on their own profile. This means that their friends get to see your update too, even if they are not a fan of your page. This is how Facebook differs from a normal website and this is how Facebook can help you get the word out about what you're doing to a large number of people very quickly.

If you're a public library and you don't have a Facebook page – get one. If your library isn't on Facebook you're definitely missing a trick. Facebook pages are free to set up and simple to control and it's easy to learn how to do it. They also have huge promotional potential and reach.

According to the Social Bakers website there are 30,393,440 UK Facebook users in the UK alone, that's 48.75% of the population – 2,646, 240 of those users live in the Greater Manchester area (source: www.socialbakers.com/facebook-statistics/cities), so for Manchester Libraries it was a no-brainer to be on Facebook. Other organizations agree – BBC Bullyproof has 59,000 fans and amazingly 90,528 people have used Facebook to check in while they shop at the Trafford Centre. So if commercial organizations and non-profits clearly appreciate the power of Facebook why should libraries be any different? How can you justify not being there?

How does FB specifically fit into your wider social media activity – does it have a particular and distinct role or style?
We also use Flickr to share photos, Vimeo to broadcast our videos and Issuu to display library brochures and guides. I blog for the library at the Manchester Lit List and we have an active Twitter account with over 4000 followers. I do share Flickr, Vimeo and Issuu content on Facebook because they are visually interesting and they are also popular with our followers. Although it's possible, I don't use our daily blog posts or tweets as automatic status updates on Facebook. I believe each platform has a different audience and engagement statistics show that Twitter followers, for instance, prefer different types of content to our Facebook followers.

I've tried to use our branding, design and content to give our page a unique 'personality'. I've worked hard to build a strong page identity and get a reputation for consistent, valuable and entertaining content. I check the Manchester Libraries page every day and respond to all comments and answer enquires online too. It's the conversation that gives our page life and it's clear that users really do appreciate the opportunity to talk to us via Facebook. I ask questions and actively seek feedback and participation because I'm aware that people want to join a community, not just another Facebook page.

You have a very impressive front page, with a bespoke banner, some embedded video and a catalogue search. Can you tell us about this?
Very rarely do fans actually visit your Facebook landing or welcome page. Most

interactions will take place on fans' own news feed, not even on our wall, but I think it's still important to have a professional-looking welcome page. Our graphics were designed by Darren Connolly, a really talented local graphic designer who did a work placement with us a few months ago. As our Facebook page hadn't yet come under the control of corporate communications I thought I'd take the opportunity to make a splash – and Darren's artwork definitely did the job.

The embedded videos give the page interest and hopefully make us stand out from the crowd. They're also another way to let people know about the changes at Central Library and the aim is to pique visitor curiosity, so that users are tempted to visit the more detailed pages of information on our website, and

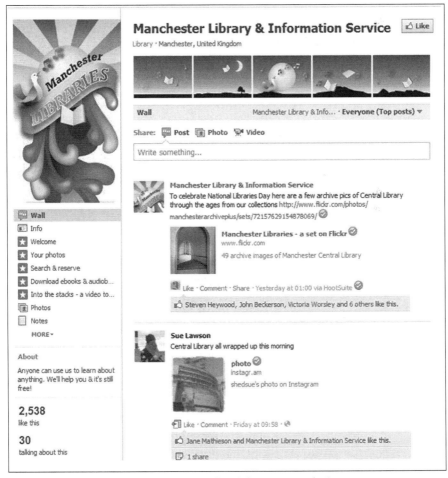

Figure 6.1 *Manchester Libraries Facebook homepage design*

website visitor metrics show that the strategy works. The catalogue search feature is simple HTML form, which I requested from our Library Management System vendor. It's worth remembering that you don't have to have a flashy landing page at all. It's more important to have an active page, to update regularly and to engage with your visitors.

Obviously a lot of work has gone into the whole FB site for the library, but presumably most users will go straight to your wall the majority of the time. How do you engage with users there?

Yes you're right – most of your fans will never return to your page once they've clicked the 'Like' button. I know I don't! They only see and interact with your content in their news feed. So how do you get your content seen in your follower's news feed? Well, it's quite an art – Facebook has something called the EdgeRank, which is a secret formula that determines who sees your updates. Increasing your EdgeRank score is also called news feed optimization and fortunately for us there are plenty of tips and articles available free online.

I've found that, unlike Twitter, content published through third party apps decreases your engagement. Keeping updates short and avoiding URL shorteners in your posts can increase your EdgeRank and updates posted outside the 9 to 5 can often get more views. Here in Manchester we've found engagement rates are highest on Fridays. Go figure!

Once you've mastered the art of the 'EdgeRank' or news feed optimization, you'll also want make sure people are interacting with your content. Don't just post 'Here is a new service' with a link! Instead actively encourage people to participate. Say 'Here's a new service – have you tried it? What do you think?' When someone 'likes' or 'shares' a library update their activity appears in their friends' news feed too – even if they are not a 'fan' of the library – and when content is shared like this there is usually a corresponding rise in page 'fans'.

We have used wall updates to help our followers, to answer questions and to pose questions. We ask for their opinions and encourage users to test new online library services. Manchester Libraries regularly post photos and videos and we've held contests and online book discussions. We post useful information and scam alerts, calls for volunteers and guest bloggers. We've hosted live chats and 'ask an expert' sessions. We are trying to connect with our users in lots of different ways, to have fun, be genuine and drive web traffic to our library website and online services. Don't post too much. We try to post once a day, twice if it's something important but do take the time to check your 'unlike' stats on Facebook Insights and discover the optimum number of posts for your followers.

Does FB play a role in reaching potential users, or is it really just aimed at those you already have?

We want Facebook to do both – to expand the library's audience and to interact with current customers. Facebook can definitely take your content to non-users of the library. This 'viral' effect, where a single message can be seen by many people by being repeated across a network of followers, is one of the major strengths of Facebook. That's why we use it – to make connections with people who'd never think of using a library, to surprise and entice potential users with our resources and also to delight, entertain and build relationships with our current customers.

Can you give us 5 top tips for developing a library Facebook page to the next level?

1 When you are starting out you want to really get momentum going and increase your fan numbers, so promote your Facebook fan page everywhere – on Facebook, online, on the web, and offline.
2 Take the time to keep people engaged by posting consistent, valuable content every day.
3 Don't be afraid to have conversations. You don't ignore people in the library so don't do it on Facebook.
4 Keep track of your posts – what's popular and what isn't and use that to create better content in the future.
5 Don't be boring – have fun!

Blogs and blogging

Institutional blogs are a great way to communicate with patrons in a way which is less formal than via press releases or the main website, but which is still the library imparting information in a way it can control.

The fact that users can subscribe to a blog is particularly attractive for the library – it's essentially a way of being invited into the user's routine on a regular basis, with new posts. Blogging is also very simple and easy – often much more so than editing the library website and creating new pages.

What to blog about?

Because they're so easy to set up and maintain, blogs can serve a variety of functions. They can specifically market aspects of the library service ('Have you seen our new . . .?') but they can also promote the library just by being a useful service in themselves. Book discussions and recommendations are perhaps the most obvious blog topic for a public library; relevant corporate news and new resources are perhaps the most obvious blog topic for a special library; how to use the academic resources on offer is perhaps the most obvious blog topic for a university or college library. All of these 'go-to subjects' have value.

Once established, library blogs can go a little deeper – for example, by offering guidance on how to use Web 2.0 technologies ('Taking your first steps in social bookmarking'), or tying in with local or national cultural events ('It's Festival season – check out our recommendations for CDs and books on music in the 21st century . . .'). You can inject a little human interest into proceedings (market the personality) by profiling librarians in blog posts, too.

The mechanics

It may be that your library already has blogging software, or it may be that you will need to create an external blog using free software. The two leading blogging platforms (as well as Tumblr, which we'll discuss separately below) are Wordpress and Blogger.

Received wisdom appears to be that Wordpress has a steeper learning curve than Blogger, but is more flexible. I would agree with this assessment, but in my opinion the learning curve isn't so steep as to be offputting, so I personally prefer to use Wordpress. Blogger is simpler to use and as it's a Google product it integrates seamlessly with many other Google tools; however, if your library blog is in any way successful, you'll probably appreciate Wordpress's increased functionality sooner rather than later.

Top tips

Here are some tips for increasing engagement with your library blog:

1 Most importantly, make it infinitely shareable. Your users should never have to think for more than half a second about how to share your blog – whether via Twitter, Facebook, e-mail, or whatever pertinent platform.
2 Make it easy to subscribe. It's easy to give people multiple ways to subscribe – and it is desirable to build up a captive audience through blog subscriptions. Blogging software will have options built in that

allow users to subscribe via e-mail or via RSS feed-readers – make sure you explain these options in plain English, rather than just putting up an image of the RSS icon and leaving it at that.

3 Make sure you're listed. Have you registered your blog anywhere? It's a lot easier for Google to find it if you tell Google it exists; same goes for other search engines. Also, stick a link on the UK Library Blogs wiki at http://uklibraryblogs.pbworks.com.

4 Get out there. Comment on other blogs as your institutional blog – people are happier to engage with you if you're engaging with others, plus it'll link back to your blog.

5 Link your social media presences. Twitter is a huge driver of traffic to blogs. Make sure you tweet a link to each blog post (depending on your target audience, you may wish to tweet one link 12 hours later too, to catch people in different time-zones – you can set this to happen automatically using services like http://future-tweets.com) and if you're lucky and others tweet a link to it, you'll get a big spike in views.

6 Put a number on it. For whatever reason, a post entitled '5 tips for doing X' will get more views than the same post entitled 'Guide to X'.

7 Ask a question. Blogs are a rare opportunity for libraries to give their users ownership of something. Ask a question, either in the title of the post or at the end, and give them a voice via the comments section.

8 Put your best foot forward at key times. If you know that you're about to experience a spike in traffic (for example because of a presentation in which you give the URL, or an article appearing with a link to the blog) then make sure there is something of really high quality and overall usefulness on the front page, to lure the new readers in and hook them . . . Then is not the time for your most recent post to be an apology about building works creating noise in the library!

Tumblr

Tumblr is a short-form blogging platform which officially counts as a 'microblog' but in practice sits roughly in the middle between Twitter and a regular blog. You can write long posts as you would on a regular blog, but more generally Tumblr is used to share short snippets, quotes, images, videos and audio. Tumblr blogs have 'followers' in much the same way Twitter accounts do, and one-click 'Re-blogging' which works much like retweeting on Twitter.

Because of its distinctive nature, Tumblr should be used by libraries in a distinctive way. Short, sharp, focused posts work best – never more than a paragraph or two long – particularly if they are on a specific theme. For example, a new materials blog listing exciting acquisitions and new collections would work well on Tumblr, as would a blog showcasing digitized images from special collections. Not all libraries will need or have use for a Tumblr account, but there are some excellent examples of those which do, at www.scoop.it/t/libraries-and-tumblr.

Google+

At the time this book is going to print, the newest social network, Google+, is just beginning to be explored by libraries as an opportunity to market to and communicate with users. The way in which Google are launching the service means it's being aimed at individuals first and foremost (with some predicting that support and functionality for institutional accounts will come later) so I don't want to take too much space here giving advice which may quickly become outmoded. One feature of Google+ I can comment on, however, is 'Circles' – this is the ability to split up your contacts on the network into different circles of friends, family, colleagues, acquaintances and so on. These different Circles then get separate and tailored information sent out to them. So for example if you wrote on your Google+ account 'I'm reading a book about marketing – what do you think is the biggest challenge facing libraries in this area?' then you might choose to disseminate that information to your 'colleagues' Circle but not your 'friends' Circle.

From an institutional point of view this is an excellent opportunity: in effect it enables segmentation, as discussed in Chapter 2. It is a really simple way to target specific information at specific groups – in a way that Facebook or Twitter, for example, don't really allow you to do. You get to decide exactly how many Circles you have and what the criteria for each are, so you can divide you users and potential users into different demographics, and market to them accordingly.

LinkedIn

LinkedIn is particularly important in the special libraries sector. Social media affords an opportunity to go where the conversation is, and business librarians in particular find that conversation often takes place on LinkedIn.

Special librarians often have less face-to-face or phone contact with their clients than a public or academic librarian may have with their users, so as ever social media is an essential avenue to explore.

In the business sector, Mary Ellen Bates (2011) advocates following (or connecting with) the employees of your company individually, and taking note of LinkedIn's status updates when it notifies you of profile changes. If you receive the 'the following people have changed jobs' e-mail and notice someone from your organization on it, send them a message of congratulations. As Mary points out, this may be the only such message they receive on LinkedIn, and will make them that much more inclined to think well of the library.

If you as an institution are connected with as many relevant users (and potential users) as possible, you're privy to more discussions to which you can contribute useful information – the upshot of which will be positive promotion of the library. It's also useful to bring people together and catalyse discussions in which you don't necessarily play a leading role, because this can lead to the library being thought of as a place that fosters useful relationships. The library as enabler is a powerful message.

Most people expect their organization to be on LinkedIn, but they may not expect their library to be there with a separate account. It's up to the library to take the initiative and make contact with the relevant people, alert them to the library's presence and persuade them of the library's value.

Conclusion

Social media is becoming more and more important every month. We have a great opportunity to go where our users are, and interact with them in a more informal way – hopefully winning a few new users at the same time. People turn to social media for information more frequently now than they did even a year ago, because every search engine brings back about a million hits too many to the queries we type in. So we ask our networks instead; we trust humans more than we trust algorithms. Libraries must be there, providing good quality information as we have always done, but across new platforms.

As a minimum, most libraries should be on Facebook and Twitter. Our users expect us to be there. We shouldn't start any social media profiles that we can't resource in the long term, but those we do should be conversational, informative and entertaining. Through social media, we can expand the audience to which we can then market the key services and resources the library provides.

For up-to-date advice on these social platforms and others as they arrive online, go to this chapter's web page: **www.librarymarketingtoolkit.com/p/ marketing-with-social-media.html.**

CHAPTER 7
Marketing with new technologies

The previous chapter covered social media in detail, but that represents only one aspect of the Web 2.0 tools which can be harnessed to market libraries and archives. Moreover, there are several other platforms, applications and new technologies which don't fall under the Web 2.0 umbrella at all, which are effective in marketing the library in this digital age.

There are two case studies in this chapter: the first focuses for the most part on those Web 2.0 tools which *aren't* considered to be social media, and comes from Aaron Tay at the University of Singapore. The second is from Justin Hoenke in the USA, who discusses his successful campaign to engage teenagers through the use of technology at the library. Individual platforms or tools covered in this chapter include Flickr, YouTube, QR Codes and Foursquare.

Quick definitions

It's very difficult to define succinctly the concepts discussed in this chapter without tying oneself in knots. If you are an uninitiated reader who previously had little familiarity with Web 2.0, I'd urge you not to worry too much about the definitions, relax, and concentrate on the practical actions this chapter recommends you undertake.

Web 2.0 refers to more recent internet platforms which are interactive, participatory or collaborative in nature. Anything which involves active contributions from the user(s), such as adding their own content or taking part in dialogue online, can be considered to be Web 2.0. Examples of this would include social media sites like Facebook, where users chat and interact, or YouTube where users upload their own videos, or employing chat functionality on a library website – they all feature user-generated content, even if that content is just typed questions from the user.

Social media, as documented in the previous chapter, describes any kind of internet platform which allows the exchange of user-generated content. Twitter is an obvious example of social media, as users are exchanging content (in this case, the written word, images and videos). By contrast, 'Ask a librarian' live-chat functionality on a library website is *not* social media (because users aren't exchanging content) but it *is* Web 2.0 (because it is interactive and participatory).

A **social network** is simply the use of social media to bring users together online socially.

It's also worth noting that **the web (or world wide web)** is distinct from **the internet** (or **the net**), in that the former refers specifically to websites, whereas the latter covers anything which can be found 'online'. This distinction is becoming more and more relevant as, for example, mobile phone apps become more prevalent – usually these are not websites, but they *are* online and are accessed via the internet. It is no longer sufficient for libraries to market on the web; we need to market across many internet platforms.

Geolocation refers to the geographical location of a mobile device. **Geolocational** apps and devices make use of the fact they're 'location aware'. More specifically, **check-ins** (a shorter version of **social check-ins**) are the act of registering (and announcing via a social media platform) that you are in a certain location. Some platforms offer rewards based on number of check-ins – check in to a specific coffee shop ten times on the geolocational app Foursquare and get a free coffee, for example.

Finally, before we start to look at specific platforms and tools, it's worth remembering that these tools come and go. New tools arrive all the time and it can be hard to assess whether they are worth library investment (certainly in terms of time, even if many of them are monetarily free). What ultimately matters – more than whether or not the tool is good or bad, even – is the *market penetration* among your users, and the opportunities the tool affords for content. If your users are moving towards a particular platform then you should be there too; if an absolutely amazing new tool emerges which you could use to promote the library brilliantly, but on a platform which is not supported or widely used by your demographic, then sadly it should probably be ignored, at least until more people are using it.

Technology works best when it solves existing problems or makes existing processes more efficient, and makes things easier for the user.

Video marketing

Marketing with video can be extremely powerful. A one-minute film can convey a lot of information about your library, in an arresting way – when done well. When done badly, video marketing certainly has the capacity to cause more harm than good.

Video sharing sites like Vimeo (www.vimeo.com) and YouTube (www.youtube.com) have helped take film-making from the preserve of the elite to the pastime of the masses. The sites will host any video you upload (providing it isn't pornographic) and it is the fact that it's so easy to *share* these videos that makes it so appealing from a marketing perspective. You can either promote a simple URL that links to the video, or you can easily embed a video within another website. Embedding is the process of taking content from one website and making it appear on another. Images, videos, slide decks and many other formats can be displayed in this way, the advantage being that you don't have to upload the content to your own website in order for your visitors to see it – you are effectively providing a window through to the original website. The only potential downside is that you are not completely in control of the content, therefore: if the original website goes down or removes/changes the content, then it will no longer display (or it will display differently) on yours.

You don't really need much in the way of technical skills to do this; the video hosting sites give you the HTML code, and you simply copy and paste it into your own site. The great thing about this process is that *anyone* can do it – so if you make a really good video, it might end up embedded in hundreds of other people's websites; a brilliant multimedia equivalent of word-of-mouth, allowing you to reach potentially huge new audiences.

There are some magnificent examples of ambitious library marketing through video – such as the Harold B. Lee Library at Brigham Young University in the USA, and their 'Study like a scholar, scholar' film, available via www.youtube.com/watch?v=2ArIj236UHs. They tapped into the zeitgeist in 2010 and released a brilliant video parodying the Old Spice aftershave advertisements which were themselves going viral at the time. Harold B. Lee's production involved 13 people including a Director of Photography, a Production Manager, a Sound Editor and so on, and was filmed on high-quality equipment – as a result it looks completely professional and is brilliantly executed. It is funny and it promotes the library fantastically well, and at the time of writing has more than 3 million views on YouTube. That is a huge audience for some positive messages about libraries. Clearly, however, the video cost a lot of money and time which most libraries will struggle to match.

So what is realistic for most libraries to achieve with video? Generally speaking, well executed and basic videos beat ambitious but poorly realized videos every single time. Quality, or lack of it, is much more apparent with a film than with just printed or audio material alone. If your video is short, punchy, informative and doesn't try too hard, it will probably be successful in promoting your library.

Tips to make a great library video:

1   You can buy High Definition video-cameras very cheaply these days, compared to the prices in years gone by. Something like an HD Flip Cam costs around £100/ US$150 and provides perfectly acceptable sound and picture quality, so if you do want to make videos it might be worth investing in one. (Flip have in the past partnered with public libraries to make them available much more cheaply for library use – Google 'Flip Camera Library Donation' to see if any schemes are currently running in your location.) You can get flexible mini-tripods which allow you to shoot at different angles whilst keeping the camera steady.

2   It is actually possible to produce excellent films using software that comes free on your computer. Windows Movie Maker on PC and Apple iMovie on Mac are certainly adequate for most library videos.

3   You can make videos without using a camera at all, of course – screen-capturing software such as Adobe Captivate (or open-source equivalents) allow you to record what's happening on your computer screen and add narration over the top. Products like Camtasia or Articulate can also act as a bolt-on to PowerPoint, to make all-singing, all-dancing slide presentations which function as stand-alone multimedia objects online. These tools are traditionally used for tutorial videos (for example, demonstrating how to access e-resources from the catalogue by showing users what to do on screen and talking them through it via the audio) but they can also be used as pure marketing tools, saving the embarrassment of a librarian having to appear on camera – showcasing features from the library website, for example.

4   If you produce a really good slide deck you can always create a video version to reach new audiences via YouTube, by importing the slides into Movie Maker/iMovie and just setting them to run for perhaps 20 seconds a slide, and adding some music if appropriate. YouTube actually

has a selection of copyright- and royalty-free music for adding to the videos you upload there.

5 Write a plan out beforehand, which details the order of shots (or screenshots if you're screen-casting). You can always change it later, but it's much easier to create a good video if you know in advance what you want to achieve.

6 It's easy to create two different versions of the same video, for different audiences. If you're segmenting your market (see Chapter 2 'Strategic Marketing') then you may have slightly different messages to put out accordingly. You don't always have to literally make two videos, you can just replace key shots or slides that define the focus of the film, and leave the rest of the content the same.

7 Leave the special effects alone! Nothing screams 'amateur video' like a completely superfluous 3D Ripple Effect on one shot of a scene, or having the first 30 seconds of your film in sepia for no reason at all. The same goes for dramatic transitions between shots, such as having one shot appear in a star-shape out of the previous one. Just because Movie Maker is capable of this wizardry it doesn't mean you need to use it! Quick fades between shots is fine, preferably effects-free.

8 Check your audio levels. It's better to sacrifice a bit of flexibility and have everyone close to the camera (assuming you're using a camera with a built-in mic) than to let people stand wherever they want for filming but then end up with a video which has to be turned up really loud in order to be heard.

9 Try producing 'One minute on . . .' videos, which are exactly 60 seconds long and focus on a different library service each time. 'One minute on . . . finding resources for your subject' at a university library, 'One minute on . . . our new kids' activities' at a public library, or 'One minute on . . . new resources' at a law library, for example. Take the one minute to explain succinctly the benefits of whatever service you describe, and leave the viewer with a link to more information at the end.

10 If you really don't want to appear on camera or use screen-capture, the other alternative is to produce something animated. Some libraries are using Xtranormal (www.xtranormal.com) as a marketing tool, creating animated videos explaining databases or working through information literacy examples.

11 Finally – when it comes to creating a video that parodies a pop music video and projects of that nature, remember that what makes librarians

laugh can also make users cringe . . . and once you've put a video onto the internet people can copy it, meaning that even if you later withdraw the film it can be there forever.

Image sharing

Various sites exist to facilitate the uploading, organizing and sharing of images online, the most used of which (aside from Facebook) is Flickr at www.flickr.com. Flickr is very easy to use and a lot of people use it, meaning it is likely to have good market penetration among your users.

Image sharing is a great opportunity to allow users to have some ownership of library content – allow them to upload their pictures to a particular collection, curate a collection of user pictures around a particular subject area, or crowdsource information about obscure material in your archives. If you have historical photographs of the region in which your library sits, then putting them on Flickr and asking users to tag them with relevant local knowledge both enriches the collections and engages the community. It's worth noting that whoever is uploading any given photo gets to set the level of copyright, from 'all rights reserved' through various Creative Commons licences, so hopefully both you and your users should be protected in that regard.

You can create photosets in Flickr – one URL with thumbnails of several related photos. This can be useful for offering a virtual 'tour' of the library (one quick tip if you decide to do this: it's simpler if you upload them in reverse order), or for recording and publicizing successful library events. Although you may store the majority of your digitized materials in a digital repository, you could draw attention to this by uploading some photographs of your special collections materials to Flickr. All of these activities are a form of library outreach.

As with all library presences online, your Flickr profile should be promoted from your main website and your other social media outlets, rather than just relying on your audience finding it on their own.

QR Codes

QR stands for 'Quick Response'. A QR Code is essentially like a barcode that you might find on a packet of food, except that it can be scanned by a mobile device – when you scan a QR Code it takes you to a specific website online.

It can also do other things, like input an e-mail address or phone number to your mobile device, but it's the web access which affords libraries the most opportunities in marketing. You can create a QR Code for any URL you wish, and it's very easy to do – a tool like Kaywa at http://qrcode.kaywa.com will generate a QR Code for any site within seconds (and for free), which you can then print on a normal printer and put wherever you think your users will see it. Another tool, www.qrstuff.com, even allows you to choose the colour.

The downside to QR Codes is that users need a smartphone with a QR Code reader or scanner to access them; these are free and very simple to use, but of course not everyone has one installed. It's up to you to ascertain whether there is enough market penetration among your demographic to justify using QR Codes or not. The upside is that they are a fresh and interesting way of persuading users to access your online content. When you scan a QR Code on your phone you are instantly taken to the website – this is quite satisfying and novel, at least for now. It is certainly quicker than typing in the URL for the site, or making a note of it to visit later.

Figure 7.1 *A QR Code for the* Library Marketing Toolkit *website*

Figure 7.1 shows what a QR Code looks like. This one took under a minute to make. If you scan this, you'll be taken to an otherwise unlisted page on the *Library Marketing Toolkit* website, containing extra questions and answers from Aaron Tay, who provides a case study later in this chapter.

Here are some tips for deploying QR Codes in your marketing strategy:

1 Consider giving the QR Code user something extra: rather than just directing the user to your library website, take them to a page which contains some kind of bonus content. It's a hard balance to get right because you don't want to exclude users who don't have smartphones – but it's possible to use QR Codes to direct the user to a page all about technology in the library, for example, or classes offering guidance on

new tools or platforms. The users who have QR Code scanners will probably be interested in this.

2 If your library has an app, offer users the chance to download it via a QR Code rather than having to search for it online themselves. QR Codes can take users with smartphones directly to the app market-place for either iPhone/iPod or Android.

3 QR Codes are a great way to integrate paper and electronic collections. My colleague Susan Clayton suggests putting QR Codes on the physical shelves above the books – these then link to the e-Book equivalent of the physical stock that sits on those shelves. If the books aren't there, the user sees a sign saying 'Scan this QR Code to be taken to the e-Book of [insert title here]' – much quicker than looking it up in the catalogue.

4 In special collections and archives, use QR Codes to offer a way for the user to find more information about the physical exhibits you have in the library, or to see more items from a specific collection.

5 QR Codes are great for linking to things you don't have the physical room to display, for example copyright guidelines next to scanners or photocopiers.

6 Create a custom URL using Bit.ly (www.bit.ly) or similar (see Chapter 5 'An Introduction to Online Marketing' for instructions on how to do this) so you can monitor exactly how many people are accessing your site via the QR Code – this is essential to find out whether it is working well as an avenue for promotion. It is particularly useful if you're displaying the same poster in multiple locations around a city: should you be paying for advertising, custom QR Codes linking to different Bit.ly URLs will make it explicit where you are getting your money's worth. Sites like http://snap.vu also provide QR Codes with built in statistics monitoring.

7 Be aware that there is the potential for fraud with QR Codes. This is low risk in libraries, but because all the square, black and white codes look much alike to the naked eye, it is possible to stick a new QR Code over the top of a legitimate one and use this to lure unsuspecting users to a bogus site. This is particularly dangerous if the bogus site is made up to look like the legitimate one, and the users enter their personal details to log-in. It is unlikely to happen in the library environment, which is traditionally free of e-commerce, but is certainly worth keeping in mind as a possibility – and certainly flag it up if a new QR Code appears to have been stuck on top of your own.

8 Finally, if you're feeling a bit more adventurous, visit

http://keremerkan.net/qr-code-and-2d-code-generator/ and choose one of the more advanced applications for QR Codes. These include the ability to open Google Maps to an exact location (fantastic for flyers promoting a library event in another venue, for example) and the ability to log users onto your library's Wi-Fi network, complete with password if necessary.

A really nice example of QR Code use can be found at Delaware County District Library – when they opened their new Orange Branch, posters featuring QR Codes were used to give patrons a way to get to know the staff by taking them to videos about each person. Shea Almont, Communications Manager, was behind the campaign:

> We received a great deal of feedback from patrons, library colleagues, and our own staff, who enjoyed the videos linked from the QR Code. We were able to really show the professional, whimsical and personable side of our librarians through high-quality design of the posters themselves as well as the videos that went along with them. Often we were told the best part of the videos were the outtakes.
>
> Our posters were both professionally printed off to 18 x 24 in. size and displayed at our new branch so those with smartphones could scan the QR Code in person. But we also promoted the posters on our Facebook, Twitter, and YouTube pages for those who hadn't yet carried the QR Code technology on their phones, but still wanted to 'participate' in viewing our campaign.

It could well be that QR Codes as a specific mechanism will be superseded by something else (Blippar at www.blippar.com, for example, is an Augmented Reality application which recognizes visual cues to trigger your phone visiting a certain URL, without the need for an actual code) but the principles above will apply to any way of quickly accessing a website on a mobile device.

Geolocational apps

As discussed in the 'Quick definitions' section at the start of the chapter, geolocational apps take advantage of the fact that smartphones and many other mobile devices are location-aware. At present the most popular app by far in this area is Foursquare (www.foursquare.com) – this can be best described as a location-based social network. Users check in to venues to

Figure 7.2 *Poster for Delaware County District Library with QR Code*

receive rewards and often these check-ins are publicized via Twitter or other networks.

The important thing to remember is that your library will almost certainly be on it already, even if you haven't set up an institutional account. If a user wants to check in to a location not yet registered on Foursquare they can create it themselves – and so your library will probably already exist on the network. People can leave tips about the location, too; these can also be just comments, negative or positive, which can be useful for the library to learn from.

Foursquare also allows unlockable achievements badges and 'specials' – this is fairly high-level stuff and it is complicated to provide incentives which users can then claim in the 'free' library environment, so I won't go into that in detail here. But it's worth noting that the person who has checked in to any given location most frequently becomes its 'Mayor' on Foursquare. So a really straightforward way of rewarding regular check-ins would be to give a prize to the Mayor – of a piece of library merchandise like a library bag for example, or if you're feeling really creative, perhaps five extra loans or free DVD borrowing for a week. This is worth doing because it encourages people to visit the library frequently, and to announce that they're doing so on a social network, increasing awareness and use. Incidentally, my advice would be not to be tempted to check in to your own library too many times; leave the 'excitement' of being Mayor to one of your users.

At a more basic level, here is a simple three-step guide to getting your library onto Foursquare – it should only take ten minutes to implement and will leave you in a much better position than before you started:

1 Claim your library. Search Foursquare.com for the name(s) of your library, and if it's there you can claim ownership of it by proving that you own it in real life. It's always worth being in charge of online information about your library, so this step is worth doing even if you don't plan to engage with Foursquare at all afterwards.
2 Add some tags. Tags on Foursquare work just like any other kind of metadata – they enable discovery. So for libraries tags can serve two functions: first, making sure existing users can actually find the library, by putting in alternative names that users might be using to search for it. Secondly, to attract potential users by adding tags that correspond to needs they might have – for example, 'free Wi-Fi', 'books', 'café', 'journals', 'archives' and so on.

3   Add some tips. Try and add some really meaningful inside information
    that rewards users for finding you on Foursquare. Let people know how
    they can find the real gems of your special collections. Tell them if you
    open longer on a certain day of the week. Let them know if you offer
    audiobooks and where they can find them. Does the library café serve
    particularly amazing almond croissants? This is the perfect place to leave
    a tip saying so! It could also take the form of a to-do list challenge for
    users new to the library and wanting to get to know it: borrow a book,
    access an electronic database to find information Google can't, read a free
    newspaper. The other good thing about writing your own tips,
    particularly for academic libraries, whose users can be somewhat
    mischievous, is that people checking in on Foursquare will see the
    library's useful advice rather than just someone's poor attempt at humour
    about the state of the first floor restroom . . .

Web 2.0 catalogues and live chat

The next case study covers more information about libraries on Foursquare,
as well as the use of Web 2.0 as part of next-generation catalogues, and live-
chat functionality on library websites.

Case study 15: New frontiers and Web 2.0 tools | Aaron Tay

*Aaron Tay, Reference Librarian at the National University of Singapore, is the
master of using technology to enhance the user experience. He believes in using
empirical data to make decisions about the library's web presence, and has a vast
knowledge of tools, technologies and Web 2.0 platforms. His willingness to share
his findings with the library community (via his blog) saw him recognized with a
Mover and Shaker award from Library Journal in 2011. In this section, Aaron talks
in detail about a whole range of useful technologies.*

**First of all, do you have any tips for libraries wishing to integrate Web 2.0 tools
with their catalogues?**
Getting item details off a catalogue onto their phones is an area libraries have
tried to solve in two ways. One involves allowing users to SMS themselves the
details. Lately, many libraries have started to embed QR Codes into their
catalogues, which allow users to scan the QR Code to get item details on their

phone. At this stage it is likely that the former will be getting more usage, because it does not require the additional step of downloading and scanning with a QR Code reader, though in certain countries like the USA there is a cost involved in receiving SMS, while in others there isn't, so this might make the SMS option more or less popular as a result. It might be a good idea to cover the bases by including both and studying the results.

Many 'next generation catalogues' like Primo, Encore and Aquabrowser include Web 2.0 features allowing users to contribute tags, reviews, ratings etc. But unfortunately those practices don't seem to have taken off. If you look at most academic libraries providing such functions, very few of their users are tagging or adding reviews and it looks very much like a empty wasteland, which hardly encourages anyone to contribute since there is no one to be 'social' with. I believe approaches like Librarything for libraries and Bibliocommon, which pull in data from all libraries in the system, are more likely to succeed, rather than standalone approaches.

Still – when it comes down to it, one must consider, why would any of our users want to contribute a review or provide a rating in our catalogues? Sure they do it in Amazon, Goodreads, etc., but such systems have the sheer numbers of users required, and provide incentives by using the data to recommend similar books or to connect with like-minded people. A recommender type system similar to Amazon's 'people who have bought this also . . .' would be a start. Incentives seem to be the key, and perhaps the idea of gamification which uses game-like mechanics to encourage desired behaviour can be employed. The LemonTree project by the University of Huddersfield is an early innovator in this area.

Are there opportunities for libraries to be involved with the geolocational side of things? Can we use the likes of Foursquare to market our libraries?

Geolocation services are still in their infancy really. While universities and libraries have used services like Foursquare, they are currently used mostly for orientation tours. But what about exploiting check-ins or its more advanced cousin geofencing? A lot of early attention in location-based services was indeed placed on game-like mechanics around check-ins as popularized by Foursquare. Doubters are saying that check-ins will never move beyond the early adopter phase and they might be right. I would say it depends a lot on local conditions. My own study of check-ins in my institution shows fair levels of use, averaging 15-20 check-ins a day, and check-ins in our library are higher than in any other venue in the university, and comparable to those of other top university libraries. I suspect a rule of thumb is that if you can get traction with Twitter, Foursquare is worth considering as well.

The main way for organizations to exploit Foursquare right now is to advertise using specials. Libraries for example have given special privileges to Mayors, you can offer 'Newbie specials' to first time check-ins, use 'Friend specials' to encourage check-ins with friends, etc. and so on. One possible use would be to have a 'Newbie special' during the first month of a new term to welcome new students.

Another option would be to register a Foursquare page where you can share tips that users will see when they check-in to locations. Some early adopter libraries which have done so include https://foursquare.com/nypl (NYPL have 37,000 followers on Foursquare), https://foursquare.com/bplboston, and https://Foursquare.com/mitlibraries.

The main catch is that the user must have followed your Foursquare page with their Foursquare account, just like they do your Twitter/Facebook account, before they see the content.

Ultimately the dream, though, is for location-based services to be merged with augmented reality and mobile such that one could select a certain location or book on a library map in one's mobile phone, and be automatically guided towards it (with a blinking cursor showing where one is in real time versus destination). While it is already possible and some libraries have done it already to hardcode a call number class to the appropriate shelf, a real-time tracking of the book is a way off.

Should libraries be utilizing live-chat functionality on their websites? If so, how should we go about doing this?
Of all the Web 2.0 tools, the one I am most enthusiastic about is live chat. Of course live chat isn't new – for example Cornell University celebrated ten years of chat reference service in 2010 – but I think the potential of live chat to both serve our users and to pinpoint weaknesses in our systems is often underestimated.

As your readers will know, the vast majority of our users will never feedback to us problems they face, and those who do through e-mail seldom mention where exactly they were when they got stuck. Embedding web chat boxes on your library pages solves this problem by giving you specific feedback on where users are when they are stuck. The nature of the questions they ask, coupled with the page they are on, often give you great insight into what they are confused about and what information is lacking on the page they are at.

At my institution we have used this to great effect to improve our FAQs, by clarifying language that confused users and by adding logical follow-up questions. Done correctly and with enough iterations your pages will start to be uncannily good at anticipating user needs.

To maximize usage, I favour an embedded web chat widget with no logins, so users can immediately type in the question as opposed to an external link that says 'chat or ask us' which opens a new page or pops up in a new window. While the former takes up more space, my experiments with different chat widget/link types show the former gets 20–50% more usage, which I attribute to the fact that many users don't want to click on a link that brings them away from their current page to a page that they are unsure will help. A hybrid way that might work is to embed a *picture* of an embedded chat box, that, when clicked, pops up in a window. Compared to a text link, the picture tells users exactly what they will be getting.

In comparison, my experience is that asking for feedback using online forms is unlikely to work. Our FAQ system currently displays an online form for users to send in queries if no hits are found and usage of that is almost non-existent. In comparison a prior version displayed a chat box, and that was drawing a respectable number of chats.

For libraries which do not have a chat service, I would recommend a limited roll-out on a subsection of pages first, to get a feel of the workload involved. I would recommend starting with adding chat functionality to FAQ pages. Users are already in a frame of mind to look for answers, so offering chat there would be logical.

Once staff are used to handling queries via chat, you can slowly expand the service by placing it on more points of need such as catalogue, databases, and advertise the service in physical spaces with posters and QR Codes.

There are both free (Meebo, AIM etc.) and paid services available, but the former tend to have a big drawback in that they are not designed to be operated by more than one operator at one time. In the paid chat service space, the two main players are LibraryH3lp and OCLC's Questionpoint, though commercial offerings like Olark, Liveperson and Zopim have been used by libraries. Depending on the size of the library, the free or low-cost options of Zopim or Olark might be sufficient.

Podcasts

Podcasts are downloadable audio recordings, usually in MP3 format – essentially like radio broadcasts, but without the need for them to have ever actually been broadcast anywhere. The name derives from the medium on which they are most often played, the iPod. They are useful marketing tools for libraries in certain circumstances, particularly because the user can subscribe to the podcast and thus sign up to receive regular recordings from the library.

Libraries are already using podcasting successfully; many of the case studies in this book mention the medium, and it can be very useful as an alternative to video or text when explaining a new feature of the library website for example, or how to use equipment in the building. You could also have 'Book of the Week'-style discussion podcasts in a public library, or 'Latest resources explored'-style updates in special or academic libraries, or 'Expert discussion'-style podcasts in a special collections context to help people engage with online exhibitions.

I wouldn't recommend investing heavily in podcasting – in fact it is very cheap to do. The sound editor and recorder Audacity is simple to use and can be downloaded for free from http://audacity.sourceforge.net. For links to information about microphones and other aspects of sound recording, see the Further Reading web page at the end of this chapter.

Wikis

Wikis are websites created using collaborative software that allows anyone to edit them – the most famous example being Wikipedia. They are, in my opinion, hugely overrated as a marketing tool. Because they're so indelibly associated with Web 2.0, wikis are often the first thing put forward as the answer to pretty much everything – 'let's have a wiki' seems to be a refrain heard in libraries across the world.

Wikis are great for their original purpose – allowing people to contribute collaboratively to a site full of information. It's easy to set up a free wiki (try PBWorks at www.pbworks.com) and they can be useful to collate patron blogs (see the section on viral marketing below), but otherwise they don't really have a role in promotion.

Slide sharing

In contrast to Wikis, I believe slide decks to be hugely underrated as a marketing tool. Every time anyone from your library presents at an internal or external event, they are in effect marketing your library. Creating good slides is easy and needn't be time-consuming, and will have a hugely positive effect on engaging the audience (both in person and online) compared with using the default templates which come with the software. Slides are also a great alternative to a static web page in terms of communicating information. It's easy to embed a presentation on your library's website, and if done well users will prefer to click through these than read through long chunks of text. Be sure to upload your presentations to Slideshare at www.slideshare.net in order to ensure maximum exposure.

Viral marketing

Viral marketing is essentially electronic word-of-mouth promotion, on a grand scale. The model can be described as marketing which is self-sustaining and self-replicating, via existing social networks. This needs certain key conditions to work. Most importantly, the content must be unusual or otherwise grab the imagination, and it must be really, really easy to share. There should be no barrier between someone happening across your marketing and being able to share it with their network.

Viral marketing is most often successful when the content going viral is an e-mail or a video; the former because they are so easy to spread to one's existing network (who in turn pass it on to their network and so on) and the latter perhaps because film captures people's imagination and because it's easy to embed video on countless websites. However, it can work with bodies of text, too, and viral marketing doesn't have to result in a million views of something in order to be a useful ploy for the library.

A really simple way to exploit this model is by asking users to blog about something library-related. Let's take a specific scenario: the promotion of 'The Big Summer Read', in which the library has selected five books which everyone should read in the summer months. Having ensured you have a *lot* of copies of each book (never market a promise you can't deliver) you could then set up a Big Summer Read wiki, using free software such as PBWorks. This wiki then links to, and is linked from, the main library website. Encourage your users to blog about each of the five books when they've read them (most wiki software will also allow people to write posts within the platform for those users without blogs, so no one need be excluded) and to link to the library wiki from these blog posts – then encourage them to add a link to their blog posts, along with their names, to the wiki itself. What then results is a self-sustaining and self-replicating marketing campaign for the library – every time someone blogs about The Big Summer Read they're exposing the concept (and the link to the library wiki) to their network, and every time someone from within that network responds and decides to take part too, they are in turn exposing it to *their* network – and this can continue to many, many levels. The audience you reach is exponentially bigger than would have been the case by promotion on the library website alone, and it takes almost no time and zero financial investment to achieve.

Technology and teenagers

The final word of this chapter goes to Justin Hoenke, who is the Teen Librarian at Portland Public Library in the USA. He's had success marketing the library using technology of the sort we haven't considered above, including video game design. His case study centres on the library as technological space, and how this can be attractive to the teenage demographic. This is a very tricky group to get in through the library doors, and Justin's unique approach has paid dividends.

Case study 16: Using technology to market the library to teens | Justin Hoenke

Tell us about how you've used technology to get teenagers engaged with your library. I understand you've used both music-making and game-designing activities to get them involved?

While both our music-making and video game design programs used technology to engage teens, the actual amount of technology involved in both of the programs was pretty minimal. Our 'Make Music at the Library' program was run by a local hip hop artist. Along with her writing skills, she also brought her own recording skills to the program. It was unlikely for my library to invest in recording software and tools, so my collaborator brought her own. She was already used to this equipment, so both making the music and teaching the teens about the actual technology came very naturally to her. For our video game design program, we actually didn't use technology at all! Since neither myself nor The Telling Room (www.tellingroom.org) had any skill in actual video game programming, we focused on where our talents lay; in the writing of the actual story, plot and characters that go into making an excellent video game.

I imagine many librarians reading this might be thinking 'I like the idea, but we can't afford that kind of kit.' Is it expensive to put together these kinds of opportunities?

That's definitely one of the things I hear a lot when I talk about these programs, but to that I say 'Guess what my programming budget is? Zero.'

The key to pulling something like this together is to find community members and organizations interested in helping out with these types of programs and to collaborate with them. Chances are, there is someone or something out there that wants to bring an awesome program like creating original music or designing video games to patrons. That's one of the great appeals to working with children or teens – that there is always a way to get them the programs they want to have because there is always someone out there desperate to work with these age-groups.

Having a video games collection might still be considered challenging (or at least, 'not what libraries should be about') by some sections of our profession – have you had positive testimonies from your local community that might convince them this is an area worth investigating?

One of the strongest 'this is why you should have video games in your libraries' stories is something I hear at least once a week while I work at the public service desk. It usually starts off with 'wow, you have video games?!' and ends with 'If I would've known this before, I would've come to the library years ago. I wish you did this when I was a teen!' I'd say that's a pretty good testimony!

I'd also like to add that it's not about the collections we have . . . it's about the people we serve. If we can't give the proper materials and services to the people we serve, then we must ask ourselves why we're even doing this. If we fail to make our communities happy, then that gives people a good reason to advocate for shutting down libraries. I'm pretty sure that's not something we want to happen.

So do you see this as a way of getting teens into the library, almost 'through the back-door' if you like, so they'll discover the books? Or do we need to be brave enough to say: gaming in libraries is an end in itself, it doesn't have to be just a stepping stone to traditional literature . . . ?

I think it can easily be about both, but I think what it all boils down to is that we reach out to all different types of people. Some people may just need that nudge to get into books, and video games might do that. For others, it may just be video games and that's it. On the other hand, we could even turn a book lover into a video gamer! In the end, video games, reading, movies and everything else are all literacy. The only thing that is different is the container in which each story is delivered.

What about the actual promotion – how do you reach teens in the first place to tell them about all this great stuff?

I believe in grassroots, word-of-mouth promotion as the best way to get any kind of word out. Once someone finds out about something cool happening in the library, it just takes them telling their parents or friends about it for it to get around the community. It may take some time (I'm just finally starting to see things I started a year and a half ago in my library take off) but the end result is great. You get people who are genuinely interested and excited about the library involved.

Earlier in the book I've talked a lot about segmentation – dividing your demographic up, and marketing differently to each section depending on their needs and wants. What is the key to winning over the teen demographic?

Talk to them one on one, treat them as unique individuals, and don't try to make things 'hip' or 'cool'. Teens can smell a phony coming from a mile away. It's best if you just be yourself and be confident. Teens have this funny way of being able to spot authenticity. Trust your gut and go with it.

Links to more how-to guides and library examples of the technologies described here, as well as information on things like Prezi and RSS feeds (for which there wasn't enough room in this chapter), can be found at **www.librarymarketingtoolkit.com/p/marketing-with-new-technologies.html**.

CHAPTER 8
Marketing and people

The previous several chapters have focused on technology, but now it is time to bring the spotlight back to those aspects of marketing that involve the Participants (from Booms and Bitner's Seven Ps model, 1981) – in other words, the people. Pitching to people, marketing with other people, reaching people remotely and utilizing other people to get your message out for you, are all pulled together and covered in this chapter. It is divided into two: Collaborating with people, and Reaching people.

There are three case studies. The first gives a really useful insight into how the media works, courtesy of journalist Rob Green. Oriana Acevedo from the State Library of New South Wales, Australia, gives some advice on marketing to multicultural communities in the second case study, and lastly Joanna Wood of Cafcass talks us through reaching remote users, on a budget.

Collaborating with people

The chapter starts with an exploration of one of the single most important techniques in marketing libraries today.

Word-of-mouth marketing

The power and importance of word-of-mouth marketing (or WOMM) are beyond dispute. WOMM is simply one or more people telling others about a product, service, institution or brand. In effect, it is the process of letting others market on your behalf, in this case by telling their friends and acquaintances about how good your library is. A certain amount of WOMM will happen without any intervention from the library: people talk to each other about good and bad experiences all the time. The aim here is to harness this as a marketing tool, and exert some kind of influence on the content of the messages going out, how they're disseminated, and who hears them.

There are countless statistics taken from research on the subject – for example that 67% of all consumer decisions are primarily influenced by word of mouth (Court et al., 2010). Customers identify word of mouth as the most reliable source for ideas and information on products and services; people prefer to use something if it's been recommended to them by someone they trust – it really is that simple. Recommending services or brands to wide audiences has never been easier than in this age of social media. So how can libraries use all this to their advantage? WOMM is quite cheap and very effective, but does require some planning and management.

Cultivate champions

WOMM has become something of a buzz-phrase in recent times, and you could be forgiven for thinking that getting person A to tell person B about your library will be the answer to all your marketing wishes. There is, of course, a lot more to it than that. For a start, you need the right person A if person B is to be truly influenced – they need to be told how great the library is by someone like them, or by someone they respect, or both. It is said that 10% of people influence the other 90%, so it's important to cultivate a library 'champion' who falls within that vital 10% to spread the word.

A technologically savvy 30-year-old who uses the library as a source of information about emerging trends and as a networking space attributes completely different value to the library than, for example, a retired person who enjoys the chance to read books about gardening in a peaceful environment. Neither would be a particularly effective advocate for the library when talking to one another, but both could be extremely effective when talking to people like themselves.

You can find influencers either by asking users (or figures within your local authority, university or business) direct, or by trying to recruit them (online or in person) via incentives. Incentives don't have to be financial or voucher-based (although that certainly works if you can afford it); the feelings of being part of something at the front line, of being able to positively influence the library, of being empowered to take some responsibility – these are all incentives, too. Dowd et al. put it perfectly in Bite-Sized Marketing (2010, 11) when they say: 'Give your influencers a VIP pass for first access to information and content. People who are involved in the process make enthusiastic influencers.' Think how much more passionate you are about your own projects than those other people ask you to work on . . . It may be worth handing over an entire campaign to the influencers, and let them try and promote the aspects of the library via word of mouth in the best way they see fit.

Susan Moore, who provides a case study on internal marketing in Chapter 9, gives this advice in recruiting library champions:

> Attend any functions you can and make sure you speak to them (but don't bore them: an anecdote about a satisfied customer works very well). Just be as friendly to them as possible, ask them about themselves and remember their first names.
>
> Ask them outright if they will help you get the word out about the library. Most people think they know what libraries do and are always astonished when they do discover what resources are there for them.

Whomever you choose, they need to have an excellent (and persuasive) communication style, and ready access to a network of potential users who would benefit from using the library if only they knew what services it could provide. And you need as many of them as you have demographics to which you would like to appeal.

Choose the messages

Once you have identified your influencers you need to work out the message they're spreading. Whether these are entirely dictated by the library or instigated solely by the influencer (or a mixture of both), the ideas you wish to communicate need to be clear and easy to grasp. Hopefully the service you wish to promote will be so fabulous it will be immediately apparent what the benefits are! To generate a buzz, it can't just be talking about the same old things in the same old way. It either needs to be a new service or resource, or a new and exciting way of communicating the value of an existing one.

Ideally the message should result in an action. It's not just about WOMM informing people how great the library website is, it's about delivering the positive review and then asking them: 'Go to page X, where there's a list of programmes they're running over the summer – sign up to one and you'll see how good they are.' Or: 'Get to the library next week while campaign Y is running and tell me what you think of it; they're bound to have something which ties in with your interests.'

Make the right tools available

The aim is to make generating a buzz around your service as easy as possible. There should be no barrier between someone wanting to tell their friends how good the library is, and being able to do so. 'ShareThis'-style buttons for online content are essential – people should only ever be one click away from spreading the word via their social network of choice. Content should be available via a number of different media to suit different types of people: printed leaflets to hand out, free gifts to distribute, videos on YouTube to watch, a dedicated page of the website. The same story, told in different ways.

Marketing and the media

If WOMM is the organic way of allowing others to tell your story, then utilizing the press is the more direct approach; the print and broadcast media represent a fantastic opportunity for free marketing and publicity for the library. While national newspapers are great for library advocacy in general, it is local papers, in particular, which offer marketing possibilities for *your* library. Public libraries can all but guarantee a significant proportion of their users and potential users will read any articles printed about them. The same applies to academic libraries, albeit to a lesser degree.

One of the key factors in successfully engaging with the media is remembering that they are all individuals with normal lives, trying to do their jobs. They don't necessarily want to put earth-shattering stories into every edition, but they *do* want to file their quota of stories without fuss, and go home at night to spend time with their families. With this in mind, when approaching the press with a potential story, making their lives as easy as possible is almost as important as providing good content.

Rob Green is a journalist with over ten years' experience working in print and broadcast news and public relations. He has also spent time as the Senior Reporter for CILIP Update magazine, the main publication from library's professional body in the UK; as both a library professional and a media professional Rob is uniquely placed to provide a case study about utilizing the media in marketing your library.

Case study 17: Engaging the local media in marketing the library | Rob Green

Gaining publicity for an event or raising awareness of issues within libraries through the media can feel like a daunting task. Journalists are busy people and will generally be working on a number of different stories at that same time while trying to meet deadlines. As in many industries, resources are being cut, meaning reporters will be working harder than ever and their time is increasingly precious. If you contact them at the wrong time it can be difficult to get your message across, as you will not be seen as a priority. However, a reporter is always on the lookout for news to report – it is the nature of the job. This means that if presented in the right way and at the right time your event or issue will, in fact, be welcomed.

Deadlines and filling space/airtime are crucial in the media. A blank page or missed deadline are unacceptable and so reporters will do all they can to prevent that from happening. Knowing this and applying some common sense to press releases or phone calls to media outlets will help you get your story picked up.

As with many things in life preparation is important and there are a few key things to consider. Deadlines exist in every media outlet the world over and for two reasons it is crucial to know when those deadlines are. First, if you have an event that takes place on a certain day at a certain time, there is no point telling the media about it if the next deadline/publication date is after the event. You will be wasting your time and theirs. Secondly, the closer journalists get to deadline day the busier they will be and the harder it will be for you to get their attention.

If you know when deadlines (and publication dates) happen you can ensure your news release is timely. If you plan well enough in advance you should be able to time a press release to hit a journalist's desk/inbox just after a previous deadline when they will be starting the search for new news and there will be a lull in newsroom activity. It is also useful to know the frequency of a publication, so that you can plan a press release to give the journalist the maximum time to deal with it, while minimizing the risk of it getting lost in an inbox or at the bottom of a pile papers. If in doubt call the news desk and ask about deadlines and publication dates – they will be happy to tell you.

Having a named contact at a newspaper should help. Try to send e-mails to an individual rather than to a generic e-mail address. If you can, give them a call before sending something – let them know you will be sending a press release and give them brief information about it. Unless they want to know more there and then, thank them and ring off. Don't forget to send the promised press release.

Once you have decided on the right time to send a release and made contact with the right people you need to ensure the content is correct. Information is key. It is your responsibility to provide full and accurate information – if the press release is wrong in any way this is still what will be published. Not only will that mean the wider public getting the wrong information, it will also mean a black mark by your name. Accuracy is what the media builds its reputation on and if you provide a journalist with the facts that are incorrect they could well decide against using your press releases in the future. They will be the ones having to deal with angry and disappointed readers and they will be the ones having to explain to their editor why there was a mistake.

Similarly, be certain to include *all* relevant information. If you want people to call to book places, include a telephone number. If it is an event make sure the start time, the date, the venue are all included. A journalist should not have to double-check a press release, so make life easy for them. A follow-up call from you sometime after the press release has been submitted can be a useful way of checking the journalist has everything they need.

When you come to write the press release, first make certain the factual content is correct, then you can think about embellishing it. Do not worry about the writing style, but be sure to be clear and concise and try to give the most important details of 'who', 'what', 'why' and 'when' in the first paragraphs. You can include a heading to highlight what you think the most important message is.

Depending on the story, you can add a quote to the press release. For an event this could be a simple 'We're sure it will be great and we hope to see lots of people there.' For a story that is more newsy you could supply a longer quote that explains the issues and shows what you want to happen as a result. Make sure any quotes avoid legalese or jargon and try to make them sound natural. If it is an emotive issue do not be afraid to show some passion!

Always include contact details – if a story is big enough the journalist may want to speak to you in more depth and will need to know how to get in touch.

If there is a chance for a photo let the journalist know, but be aware that pictures of faceless chief executives or politicians do not sell newspapers so there is very little point asking for a photographer if the local Mayor will be the only person in attendance. Celebrities and children are always good and there is no need to worry about so-called data protection issues with children. Newspapers know media law better than you and should always make sure the correct permissions have been sought for photographs.

Finally, it's important to be resilient. Time and space are finite and so you need to be aware that not everything will make it into the paper. A journalist will never promise anything because they know how quickly things can change. Remember that it is not personal if your story does not make it, so do not take it personally and keep on trying.

Cross-promotion

This is the final strand covering collaborating with people to promote the library. Outside the world of libraries, cross-promotion is increasingly important in marketing – particularly with so many marketing budgets feeling the pinch. In short, cross-promotion is the process of allying your organization with another (complementary) organization, and promoting yourselves together. The benefits are that you can share promotional costs, and ideally reach markets via each other which you couldn't reach on your own. A really basic example would be that your library forms a promotional alliance with the local museum. You promote the museum via your social media feeds, and the museum does the same for you; essentially you are bartering for free advertising. Neither organization incurs any cost, but both benefit from having their brand exposed to a naturally sympathetic audience.

Some tips for cross-promotion:

1 Your reputations are linked through this process too, so choosing a suitable partner is essential.
2 Cross-promotion can happen with more than one other organization, boosting your access to new markets even further.
3 In the world of social media, advertising is no longer essential. However, you can halve the cost of an advertisement in the local paper if you take one out together with another organization.
4 Set up displays in each other's premises. To take the museum example: the museum could display some special collections materials which support a particular exhibition, and the special collections department could display relevant museum artefacts alongside printed materials in return – each with flyers for customers to take away, giving more details of the institution.
5 Run a competition jointly – for example, a prize draw for people who sign up to both institutions' mailing lists, the prize for which could be a behind-the-scenes guided tour of both buildings.
6 In a slight variation on the theme, some libraries have been able to offer services in exchange for free advertising – for example, digitizing a company's business records in exchange for their promoting the library locally.

Reaching people

In order to reach your target audience, you need to be able to communicate with them appropriately. An area of market research and strategy on which there is very little advice and coverage already available is marketing to multicultural communities. Oriana Acevedo is the Multicultural Consultant at the State Library of New South Wales in Australia and has run successful campaigns in this area; she details them in this second case study of the chapter.

Case study 18: Marketing to multicultural communities | Oriana Acevedo

What are the first questions we should be asking ourselves, when planning marketing to multicultural communities?

What do you know about the community? How large is the group, what language(s) do they speak? What is the age breakdown of the community? What are the literacy levels? What are the cultural dynamics of the community – e.g. are women likely to speak? How do they travel to work – e.g. do they drive/use public transport? Does the community you are targeting have any knowledge or experience of a free public library as a concept? It is important to start with the community needs, build library services and collections from their perspective; don't just market existing collections to them.

How do we meet these challenges?

It is not about having a unique multicultural marketing strategy. Everyone needs to think about it as part of their role (building collections, developing programs, communication, customer service, organizational capacity and marketing).

Some key points:

- It is very difficult to market from the outside into a community – we find it is important to join in with existing networks and form partnerships.
- Identify multicultural workers within the community (e.g. migrant resource centres, health workers) and work with them.
- Choose models from the community for advertising material.
- Marketing materials need to be representative of the people in the community (e.g. older, younger, professionals, stay-at-home).
- Use speakers from the community (for video/media/events).
- Target the multicultural media (e.g. Vietnamese health collections via Vietnamese community radio and newspaper).

- Advertise in places the community frequent (e.g. public transport billboards, bus stops, churches and religious venues).

You ran the successful MyLanguage project.

MyLanguage is a national internet portal designed to deliver information and complement library services to multicultural Australia using a number of innovative web-development techniques and scripting languages. The marketing of the MyLanguage involved banners, bookmarks and YouTube videos in multiple languages.

In June 2008, on behalf of the national partnership, the State Library of NSW recruited over 30 native speakers, representing a wide range of languages, to participate in the filming of video clips. In total 34 different videos, each of approximately 1.5 minutes in duration, were individually scripted by the native speakers to emphasize library services in a culturally appropriate manner. Within the first year the portal had been visited almost 10 million times. By August 2008 it was getting over 1.5 million hits per month.

Do you have any more practical advice as to how other libraries can market to diverse communities?

- Radio interviews talking about the services (on community radio)
- Be proactive in networking with the community
- Be very positive/certain in your approach to a community
- Projects take about two years to become effective and raise awareness in multicultural communities – be patient and don't give up.

An additional full case study from Oriana, covering the MyLanguage Project in more detail, is available on the website: **www.librarymarketingtoolkit.com/p/case-study-mylanguage-internet-portal.html**.

The elevator pitch

A key aspect of reaching your library's key influencers is being ready to deliver the perfect pitch when the opportunity arises. An 'elevator pitch' is a promotional speech, around 30 seconds long, which you should have ready to deliver any time you meet a library stakeholder or potential library stakeholder. The name derives from the idea that should you find yourself in an elevator (or lift) with the boss or client of your dreams, you should be ready to pitch a tightly focused list of reasons why they should employ or hire you by the time you reach the ground floor; it is more often associated with marketing oneself than one's institution. However, I believe it can be hugely valuable for marketing libraries rather than merely individuals, and moreover I believe that *not* having a good pitch prepared can actually cause harm rather than just represent a wasted opportunity. Think of the last time you asked someone about their business or profession and they failed to give a good account of themselves: you probably left the conversation with less inclination to investigate that business in future.

So, a library elevator pitch needs to briefly but compellingly lay out the value of the library in question. It will be useful when talking to important people like academics (in university libraries) members of local government (public libraries) or business partners (special libraries) but it will also be useful when talking to *anyone* – converting several individuals into library users over a long period of time is a valuable exercise.

Here are some essential tips for preparing yours:

1 Make it short. Even though this is a pre-prepared speech it is something you are going to be slotting into normal conversation; as such, it can't be much more than 30 seconds long including pauses, erms and ums.
2 Rather than building from the ground up with contextual information, go straight in with the most important piece of information about your library (which should be tailored to the audience you're talking to).
3 No jargon, no acronyms: speak their language. Think in terms of benefits to them.
4 Give them enough information to make them curious, rather than telling them everything all at once – the idea is to inspire them into wanting to prolong the conversation, and then you can tell them everything else . . .

It's also worth pointing out that you can turn the whole elevator pitch concept on its head, and use an equivalent opportunity to find out all about the person you're talking to. Rather than trying to sell the library at this first meeting, you can use it to get information about how the library can best serve them in future, and build from there. Rebecca Jones calls it the 'elevator listen':

A chance encounter with a decision-maker is a fantastic opportunity to hear about them – what are they working on? Where are they headed today? Have they ever heard of the information centre? You don't have to stick a microphone in their face and pepper them with questions, but showing interest in people – finding out about their work – is the basis for all good relationships. Then at the next conversation, you can start to align the library's services with their role, their experiences, etc. Position the information services with their work in a meaningful way – a way that has meaning for them because it fits with what they are doing.

Reaching remote users

Finally in this chapter, we look at reaching remote users of the library – at little or no cost. In the academic and special library worlds in particular, remote users make up a significant percentage of library users, so it is vital to market to them effectively and ensure they feel valued. Joanna Wood is the Librarian at the Children and Family Court Advisory and Support Service (Cafcass) which is a Non-Departmental Public Body in the UK, and has had great success reaching users who can't visit the library in person. She takes us through her techniques here.

Case study 19: Marketing a remote library service on a budget | Joanna Wood

First of all, how do you use e-mail and the internet to reach remote users?

I produce a monthly 'Recently Added to the Library' bulletin, which contains bibliographic information and a brief abstract for each book, journal article and online publication that is added to the library catalogue in the previous month. Each bulletin contains 100–200 items and is e-mailed as an attachment to 294 Service Managers (social work managers) with a note to cascade it to all staff. The e-mail also contains a prompt to remind social workers that we can do subject searches and produce resource lists.

The library has a page called 'Library Zone' in the organization's monthly e-bulletin. The page is split into two: library news at the top (e.g. library developments, brief 'How to . . .' guides and tips and tricks) and brief info on a few new publications at the bottom, which usually have a theme: e.g. shared parenting; contact with birth parents after adoption, etc.

The library has a presence on the staff intranet. The purpose of the library intranet page is to provide a link to the library catalogue along with the contact details of the library staff – invaluable when you run a remote service that has moved offices three times in the last two and a half years! There is also a news sidebar, links to the 'Recently Added . . .' archive (maintained on a sub-page) and a complete list of our journal holdings, along with login and password info for our institutional subscriptions. There are also links to the library policies: our Service Level Agreement, Collection Management Policy and Communications Policy and a Library FAQ guide. We sit near the Communications team and they come to us for leads on news items for the intranet, e.g. new publications, and I ask that they put a link to the library in the piece or the unique item number on the library catalogue so that people have to ask us for it.

I make sure that the library catalogue link is extremely visible. It's in the e-mail signatures of the library staff (with a reminder to 'visit the library catalogue') on the home page of the intranet, and the library pages of the intranet. I also encourage people to bookmark the catalogue homepage in their Favourites folder.

You use 'library champions' to spread the word – how do you cultivate these, and how important is word of mouth in reaching remote users?
The 'library champions' are based around the organization (we have around 80 offices in England) and have very kindly taken it upon themselves to promote the library on our behalf. They are usually very satisfied library users and/or pro-active Service Managers. They get every single member of staff on their team or in their office to use the library – some have even been known to raise library use in supervision with their social workers as part of a commitment to evidence-based practice.

Word of mouth is a crucial part of the library's success. One person in an office (say, Leeds) orders an article from the library. They're impressed with the quality and speed of service and recommend it to their immediate colleagues. The next day we get a deluge of requests from people in the Leeds office. Our statistics show that once someone joins the library, they are likely to use it again at least four times in a year.

I imagine reputation must be very important when dealing with remote users – you can't always speak to them directly, so the actions and perceptions of the library have to speak for you.
We live and die on the speed and quality of service we provide. We're used to the curveball enquiries, the 'needle in a haystack' searches, the 'hard-to-get' requests. If the obvious channels don't yield a result, I'll contact the professor who wrote the research (even if they're now based abroad) or the relevant subject librarian at the university that funded the research and we'll find a way to get the ancient article, the out-of print-book or the no-longer-available-online literature review.

We've built up a reputation for getting things quickly and for being reliable and comprehensive as a result.

I'm also very proud of the work that we do to support continued professional development. If a social worker is doing a Masters degree or Post-Qualifying course, we encourage them to give us their reading list and we'll get the resources if we don't already have them. Writing a literature review? We'll start them off with a subject search. We also have guides to writing essays, dissertations and the Harvard referencing system in the library. As a result we sometimes get thanked in dissertations and theses!

Have you tried anything that didn't work, any lessons to impart?
I used to visit individual offices and do a brief talk during their staff meetings and offer at-desk training. This was less successful (sometimes people were interested, sometimes they weren't) and it was too time-consuming to do with relatively little benefit. This is an object lesson in trying something out, finding it didn't work and abandoning it.

Tell us about the '400 project'.
We have around 1450 front-line social work staff in the organization and 1050 of them use the library. My current obsession is trying to work out why 'the 400' don't use the library. I e-mailed them a gentle reminder that the library exists, along with the most recent 'Recently added . . .' bulletin and a 'Recently published . . .' bulletin, and an outline of the services that the library can provide, just to give them a flavour of what we do. The 400 have been recorded in a spreadsheet and each time we 'hook' someone into using the library their name is removed. I have to accept that 'you can lead a horse to water . . .' but we have picked up quite a few new users since I sent out the e-mails.

Finally, what's the most important advice you can give to someone wanting to market their library to people who will very rarely come to it in person?
If the product works, marketing it is easy. We have set up a very simple remote ordering system and made ourselves as visible as it is possible to be when running a remote service with no marketing budget. If we haven't got something in the library, we'll find it or buy it in (within reason). Our turnaround times are quick. Our aim is to make the social workers' lives as easy as possible when it comes to accessing relevant, timely research and information.

We provide a library service to demanding, exacting, time-poor, knowledge-hungry people and we do it extremely well.

For more information and further reading, including lots more on the MyLanguage Project, go to **www.librarymarketingtoolkit.com/p/marketing-and-people.html**.

CHAPTER 9
Internal marketing

This chapter covers two related aspects of marketing which are increasingly important in libraries, but have not been discussed or written about often enough: marketing *to* internal stakeholders, and marketing *with* internal stakeholders.

The importance of internal marketing

Internal marketing really means promoting the value of the library to the wider organization in which it sits, be that local authority, business, or university. An internal stakeholder can be defined as an individual or group with a legitimate investment in the success or otherwise of the library; an external stakeholder would usually be the customer. Unlike the customer, however, someone with a contractual or economic interest in the library may both seek to influence the marketing process, and *be* a market themselves. In my view, the importance of marketing to internal stakeholders is massively undervalued in the library community – I see it as an essential use of our time. These people hold the purse-strings for our libraries, and it is they who can wield the axe in tough economic times; the aim should be to market ourselves so well to them that the need to promote a campaign among our users to 'save our library' never arises. Because, whilst the users are absolutely essential, they don't ultimately decide whether or not to invest money into the library service (although they can certainly help persuade those that do). Rosemary Stamp, a marketing consultant who works closely with libraries, provides an expert view on communicating messages to an internal audience in the first case study of this chapter.

Another use for marketing to internal stakeholders is to be allowed to generate forward-thinking initiatives. We need to be promoting our successes to our bosses in language they understand – particularly if our bosses are not librarians – in order to secure a mandate to innovate. Andy Priestner of Cambridge University provides a case study on this subject.

Increasingly, libraries have to market themselves in collaboration with others – this presents a whole new set of challenges, including the tricky business of marketing within wider institutional branding guidelines, as discussed with Susan Moore of the ICAEW Library in the final case study of this chapter.

Marketing *to* internal stakeholders

Proving the value of the library to the people who matter is a never-ending task. It's also very difficult, but certain tools and techniques are available to us which can help persuade internal stakeholders to subscribe to our point of view. We'll look at some of them here.

The stakeholder audit

Conducting an audit of internal stakeholders is in essence an inward-facing version of the market research and segmentation discussed in Chapter 2. It is the process of identifying who the key internal stakeholders are, how important they are, what their needs are and how you will meet these.

It may be useful to use a variation of a risk analysis model to determine the strategic importance of each stakeholder. A basic risk analysis grid contains two factors for each eventuality or risk it describes: how likely it is, and how great a negative impact it would have if it happened. Something which scores highly in both categories (an event which is both likely and has far-reaching consequences) is considered high-risk. For the internal stakeholder, the equivalent two factors are first how interested the person is in the library, and secondly how influential they are on its future.

If you were to score each category out of ten, then anyone scoring ten or above out of 20 in total will need particular attention as part of your internal marketing efforts. Anyone very interested in the library must be kept onside, as must anyone highly influential. It may help to draw up a table of stakeholders as part of the audit, which includes those scores, as well as other essential information such as their needs and, ultimately, library strategies to fulfil them. Table 9.1 is a much-reduced example, for a fictional legal library.

Having audited your stakeholders and decided on the appropriate messages for each, the next stage is to communicate those messages successfully.

Table 9.1 *Example of a table of stakeholders*

Stakeholder	Interest rating	Influence rating	Combined score	Current needs	Marketing strategies
James Senior Partner	4	8	12	Competitive intelligence	James is happy with the library, if not overly interested, but highly influential in the firm. We'll aim to increase his engagement with the library by offering to brief him in new developments in his specialist field via Skype, as he often works off-site.
Debbie Senior Partner	8	7	15	Specialist database knowledge	Debbie is not only influential but has a very positive attitude towards the library. As such we'll develop her as a 'library champion', providing the specialist knowledge she requires and the tools to spread the word of the library's success.
Craig Junior Solicitor	7	1	8	Case law	Craig uses the library a lot, but he's an intelligent person who doesn't like feeling stupid or asking too many questions. As he is of low influence we'll make him aware of our social media channels so that he gets the information he needs without having to ask directly, and can be marketed to without a large time investment from the library.
Michelle Marketing Manager	2	10	12	For the library to make the company look good	Michelle isn't interested in the library at the moment, but as the Marketing Manager she has a big influence. Market library success stories to her in bite-sized format that she can easily incorporate into her own marketing.

Internal communication

Effective internal communication is one of those areas of professional life that becomes instantly easier as soon as one has a little guidance on how to achieve it. Rosemary Stamp is Director and Principal Consultant of Stamp Consulting (www.stampconsulting.co.uk) and she provides a case study on the ten rules of success; these are easy to digest and act upon. Rosemary advises private, public and education sector organizations on strategic marketing, brand competitiveness and positioning, policy response and strategic planning. She facilitates competitive briefings and strategic planning programmes for executive boards throughout Europe and has led competitive brand positioning strategies for a wide range of public and education sector organizations.

Case study 20: Effective internal marketing and communications – ten rules of success | Rosemary Stamp

The effective management of internal marketing and communications is critical to successful communication with a diverse range of internal audiences, in 'noisy' and complex organizations where a multitude of voices must compete to be heard.

Successful internal marketing and communications management is all about targeted contact and accurate communication:

- which will enable your key audiences to understand the relevance that your services or initiatives may have for them, compared to others on offer
- which gives your internal audiences reasons to listen to, or prioritize, your communications, against alternative demands seeking their attention
- which enables your target audiences to make informed and confident choices about the services or initiatives that you communicate through your messages.

The 'ten rules of success' will help you to identify and overcome potential barriers and plan your internal marketing and communications effectively.

1 Identify and target your internal audiences

It is critical to get information about your services, priorities or activities to the 'right' people within the organization, rather than simply attempting to contact everyone (and anyone) randomly. This will include not only reaching those that will use the services that you provide, but also those that influence your target stakeholders – plus those that might make decisions or expenditure on their behalf (or yours). In this way, it is just as important to know who will *not* be interested in your activities, plans and services as it is to know who *will* be likely to use them or exert an influence over them, in some way.

2 Communicate at the right time

Internal communications to your target audiences need to be aligned with their planning and decision-making schedules. For example, if you need people to sign up for your initiatives and programmes or to support your budget or planning bids, it is vital to plan ahead to make sure your communications will reach them in time to inform their choices and enlist their attention and support, rather than reaching them too late, when decisions have already been made. If you need people to commit to expenditure, be sure you know when they make decisions about budgets and resource allocations. In your internal marketing and communications planning process, the management of lead times for implementation or activity will be fundamental to success.

3 Use the right communications channels

Which communications channels or modes will work best? Will your target audience respond best to informal or formal communications? Do they prefer reports and papers, e-mail, social networking or personal contact? Which forums will be the most useful to you? Make sure you have a voice (or a knowledgeable and supportive 'champion' to speak on your behalf) at any relevant committees or working groups.

4 Speak their language

Remember, in-house or specialist terms that you understand may mean nothing to your target audience. It is vital to communicate using the language and terminology with which they are familiar. Avoid jargon and acronyms; make sure that communications are not too 'insider-focused', but have resonance for the target audience and can be understood easily.

5 Market the benefits

Use a sound proposition for the services, plans or initiatives that you wish to promote: avoid communicating just the features of 'what we do', but market the benefits that the services or initiatives will provide for others. Give your target audience a reason to value or prioritize your service, and to pay it the necessary attention, over any others that may compete for their interest.

6 Match your services or plans to a specific need

Make sure that your services or plans are relevant. How do they respond to a specific stakeholder need? How might they solve an emerging problem? In what way are they important to the interests or concerns of your target audience? Without obvious factors of relevance in your messages, your audience may just fail to be interested in what you have to say.

7 Advance test your internal marketing and communications

While we might believe that our marketing or communications plan is bound to be a success, it is always wise to test it out in advance on a sample of recipients. This can save money and time and enable you to fine-tune internal marketing and communications plans to ensure the best possible return on the efforts that you make.

8 Use a 'call to action' to engage your target audience

Internal marketing and communications activity should always aim to stimulate a response and encourage people to get involved (otherwise you will be simply making announcements, which your audience may choose to ignore). What incentive to get in touch with you and follow up would work best for your target audiences? Including a call to action will also enable you to monitor response levels to your marketing and communications activity, a critical factor in evaluation (see point 10).

9 Response management

If you want internal audiences to respond to your marketing and communications, it is imperative that effective systems are in place to cope with resultant incoming enquiries. Make sure that e-mail and telephone contacts are monitored and answered effectively. If this does not happen, there is a risk that the audience's interest will fade before they have found out more about the services or plans being promoted: they will also be much less inclined to pay attention when you communicate with them, next time.

10 Evaluation

Always evaluate the results of your internal marketing and communications effort. This will help you to refine your plans, manage budgets or time and enable you to improve activities next time around. What was well received by your target audiences? What generated the highest call-to-action response? What worked well? What did not work? What would benefit from improvement?

You will notice that if you take the above ten tips in isolation without their explanations, they would really apply across the board – to external as well as internal marketing. This emphasizes a key point: marketing to internal stakeholders is just as vital, and should be taken just as seriously and practised as thoroughly, as more traditional outward-facing marketing.

Telling stories, proving success and marketing upwards

Sometimes there's nothing like raw, hard data to prove success; the key is to provide statistics that reflect what is important to the internal stakeholders, rather than necessarily what is important to the library. You'll often hear people say that it's important to tell a story; statistics are even more powerful when paired with a story. Elizabeth Elford (who provides a case study in Chapter 10), states:

> Statistics are important. They have a place. But they need to be paired with powerful and personal case studies from and about people who are benefiting from libraries. Statistics alone are never enough. But case studies alone aren't, either. Ideally, the industry would use the statistics to back up their case studies.

Stories engage people and leave a lasting impression that numbers and facts cannot. So how do you tell a story about your library? It's helpful to think in terms of plot and characters. Your success story should have a beginning, a middle, and an end, clearly showing the context in which the library succeeded and the impact this had.

For example, let's say you launched a new service at a business library, providing an electronic summary by e-mail of new developments in the field. Client X used to have to go through paper lists and summarize new developments themselves as part of their working day. The short version of this story is: 'We launched a new service, working on your behalf, to save you hassle and time.' The storified version is: 'Client X used to have to spend an hour each day wading through paper reports to keep on top of their game. The library identified that this was something they could do on the client's behalf, using their excellent information skills – they are information professionals, after all. The library stepped in and produced an electronic version which they e-mail to the client at exactly 4pm each Monday, because that's when the client is travelling between offices and therefore has time to read e-mail on their smartphone. The time saved by being able to read the e-mail summary on the go allows Client X to get home and spend an extra hour with their kids every Monday.' This story has a beginning to frame it, a middle where the library steps in to help, and an end where Client X has a tangible gain which most of us can identify with.

Stories help those unfamiliar with libraries contextualize the work we do. There are many, many examples of libraries across all sectors whose actual boss or chief executive is not a librarian and so cannot be expected to understand success using the same criteria as an information professional might use. Andy Priestner is Information and Library Services Manager at Cambridge University's Judge Business School, and he uses the next case study to discuss marketing upwards to non-librarians, channels of communication for internal stakeholders, and proving success.

Case study 21: Marketing upwards | Andy Priestner

I think an oft-neglected area of marketing in libraries is marketing within your own organization. How important is it to market upwards (to the people in charge) in order to be able to innovate?

It is hugely important to market upwards to senior managers, especially if they are not librarians themselves. Putting your efforts into delivering a tremendous all-singing, all-dancing library service is all well and good but if you do not have senior management understanding, or buy-in, then you and your service are sitting in the firing line. Whether we like it or not, those who don't understand what we do or value what we bring to an organization see us as a soft target – a quick way of reducing deficits when they arise. Unless you go out of your way to tell them differently they will automatically assume that you are doing things the way libraries have always done them. Of course, their previous experience may not be limited to the 'stamp, shelve and shush' model, but it is safer, if depressing, to assume this to be the case. It has been my experience that most senior managers, however intelligent, personable or charming, have little or no understanding of what it is librarians do today.

As far as senior managers are concerned, libraries and innovation are not obvious bedfellows, so that means there is a bigger hill to climb to begin with: not only do you have to convince them to allow you to take the service in an innovative direction, but you might have to convince them that librarians should be innovating at all, and that means going back to basics and explaining our purpose and role as information providers in simple terms. This message should be couched in terms of service and support rather than products or process. You need to be ready to repeat this message consistently and at regular intervals until you feel the message has hit home and, even when you think it has, I'd advise to repeat it some more. It is amazing how readily senior managers will internally reset to their default clichéd understanding if we, or the library service, drop under their radar for too long. You should seek to foster a long-term relationship with these people, not only to ensure they remain on message but in order that they think of you in informed terms when budgets are threatened or more positively when organization-wide projects or opportunities arise in which you and your service could potentially be involved.

Typically, those in charge don't have either the time or the inclination to notice, let alone absorb, your marketing strategies, so you need to ensure that you target them in a specific and personalized way. Ideally, you need to prove the library's relevance to them as individuals before you start to hold forth on the relevance of the library service to the wider organization. Maybe ask them how they access the day-to-day information they need, or try to establish if there are any gaps that your service can fill?

It is not enough, though, for those in charge to rubber-stamp your strategy. You will also need to convince stakeholders lower down the chain that it is in their interest too, otherwise they may well feel that you have 'gone over their heads' in order to get your way and this will lead to lack of co-operation, leaving you unable to implement your ideas regardless of the fact that you have won senior management support.

When it comes to the services and strategies that you want to implement, you need to be able to prove to senior management that they are aligned with the mission and objectives of the organization. You should not be thinking about your service in isolation but forwarding a more inclusive inter-departmental 'bigger picture'. Innovation which involves collaboration for the greater good of the organization is unlikely to be rejected.

Having said all that, true or natural innovators will not wait for committees or individuals to run their ideas up the corporate – or in my case academic – ladder; they will identify relevant strategies and implement them. Yes, we need to market upwards but we should not stand idly by while we're waiting for the people up there to understand us or say yes to us; after all, actions speak louder than words (and some managers may never say yes). More than anything else it will be evidence of demand or of past successes that will encourage them to support you in future activities.

What are the best channels for marketing to internal stakeholders?
In one sense every channel. I do take a bit of a scattergun approach when it comes to ensuring that the service is understood because I believe the message bears continual repetition and reinforcement. Conversely, however, I also believe in personalizing library services to individuals, so with key people it is worth identifying not only the appropriate channels but also the appropriately worded message for them to receive. Of course it is no good using the same style of message for every channel, it must be adjusted for the platform you are using as well as the audience.

The most disastrously over-used channel of our time is e-mail. In point of fact I think we could all significantly improve our marketing communication in one fell swoop by simply pledging not to use it as much as we do. In pursuit of 'inbox zero' today's stakeholders will guiltlessly delete generic e-mails from library staff regardless of their content. We need to stop wasting our time carefully composing beautifully worded e-mails and wake up to this fact. Even if we get lucky and a 'library e-mail' is read, it is highly likely that it will be skim-read rather than inwardly digested, particularly if it is longer than a few sentences. Our services our complex, but if we're going to use e-mail at all we must ensure our messages are not. Strip them of the jargon and the detail and cut to the chase.

A channel that is also widely misused is the dreaded 'library poster'. We live in a highly visual age in which compelling images and brands seek to grab our attention at every turn. We librarians can either choose to compete with the big boys and grab some 'screen time' for ourselves or we can continue to trot out the same tired and, more importantly, unread text-heavy posters which tend to resemble drab PowerPoint slides. We can make our content stand out by using bold full-page images and straplines. We can go digital and utilize display screen technology so that we are offering a continuous stream of information rather than just one static poster. We can use QR Codes to direct users to our content on their smartphones. All of the above should be consistently branded too. And that doesn't mean slapping a logo on every poster but instead ensuring that our messages communicate our values. Above all our visual messages should be attention-grabbing, professional and, if at all possible, aspirational.

Social media channels are another valuable means of connecting with internal stakeholders. We have found that this connection has not been forged through individual posts and tweets, but due to our promotion of the fact that we are on these platforms and understand how they work. My team and I regularly offer our expertise and support to help faculty and staff to, for example, start blogging, or to use Twitter in their research. Not only is our assistance greatly appreciated but their perception of both our skills and remit expands as a result.

Of course, the most effective channel we can use is direct communication because via this medium we have a higher guarantee that the message has been received and understood; better still, it can mean genuine two-way dialogue – a fertile basis for discussion as to how we can assist and support the stakeholder in question. I try to ensure it happens as frequently as possible and have found the simplest means of achieving it is to spend more time sitting working in public areas where I can be seen. Visibility is absolutely key to marketing success and the principal reason why I set up a staff information point in our busy staff and student common room. Like 95% of our electronic resources, we staff are also now available beyond the library walls and that is how it should be.

Do you have any mechanisms you use for recording and measuring the success of new ideas/implementations?

I take statistics on everything that moves, and some things that don't. This is because I once worked for a library service which did not record them enough and when we were asked specific statistical questions by senior management, and we did not have them at our disposal, the future of our service was placed in serious jeopardy. I vowed never to be in that position again and moreover to make sure that the statistics taken record our value and relevance and could, if necessary, help to fend off proposed cuts to the service.

My most important tool for communicating and recording the success of my service is my annual report, which is unashamedly an exercise in marketing and propaganda. That's not to say its contents are not true, but instead that it is presented in such a way as to maximize understanding and appreciation of our offering and achievements. In a way I suppose it's my way of saying 'Hands off – we're doing fine.' It also communicates my service strategy and where we are headed next, proving that librarians and libraries can be just as innovative as other departments or functions, if not more so.

Language

Using appropriate language is essential. More specifically, speaking *their* language is essential. This means not just using the terms that matter to the people you're talking to, but framing the story you're telling them in a context that appeals to them. (This also goes back to the guiding principle from Chapter 1, of describing benefits, not features.)

Let's take a specific example: a university library tagging its entire collection with RFID during the vacation. Many libraries have added or are in the process of adding Radio Frequency Identification (RFID) tags to their books, allowing issue and return without the need to scan a barcode. This is a huge undertaking, it takes a lot of time and organization, but the benefits are many. If the librarian reports to senior management within the wider university that 'The library has tagged over 30,000 books with RFID this summer' then they're not marketing this achievement successfully. It is jargon-heavy (RFID doesn't mean anything to most non-librarians), it gives a statistic without the context that makes it impressive (30,000 books have been tagged – is that good, did it take long?) and, most importantly, it isn't an achievement that the senior management will have any reason to value. They simply don't know enough about it to see why it should be celebrated. A better way to present the same information might be to say: 'We've introduced some new technology to our collections, which allows for quicker and more automated check-in and check-out of materials; this has freed up staff to add value to our services elsewhere.' Then the senior managers may better understand why this is to be celebrated. It scarcely does justice to all the work you as the librarian know went into tagging 30,000 books, but it allows the senior managers to feel that the summer has been spent making the library newly efficient, using new technology. This appeals to them.

Speaking your stakeholder's language extends to body language, too. Face and hands are key to engagement when conversing with people, particularly successful people, which makes Skype or other video-conferencing software a better alternative to the phone when you are attempting to build relationships with those who, ultimately, are the key investors in your library.

The language and the values of your internal stakeholders vary between sectors, and it's up to you to identify what is important to the people with whom you're communicating. Stephen Abram has said about working in special libraries (versus the public or academic sectors) that the difference is '... you're dealing with highly intelligent adults, who don't like to admit they don't know stuff. So they ask questions as instructions – and the challenge is to "answer" without embarrassing them.' (Abram, 2011b)

Marketing *with* internal stakeholders: co-operative promotion

Marketing within wider guidelines

One of the most challenging aspects of marketing with third parties is working within strict guidelines laid down by the parent organization of the library. Be it university, council, government or business, that parent organization will probably have its own branding, house style and ideas on how the library needs to conform in these areas.

It is still possible to innovate and to market successfully under these conditions, as this next case study from the special libraries sector illustrates.

Case study 22: Marketing within strict branding guidelines | Susan Moore

The Institute of Chartered Accountants in England and Wales (ICAEW) has had a library in continuous existence since the 1870s, and the library is listed among the principal benefits of membership of the organization. Library staff handle over 18,000 enquiries each year, and the website gets well over 1 million visits. The library represents a success story in terms of integrating its own marketing with the goals of the wider organization – it has to market itself in conjunction with ICAEW as a whole, working with marketing executives and promoting the service within the company guidelines. Head of Library and Information Services Susan Moore explains how they work successfully in a co-operative environment.

First, can you describe some of the main challenges of marketing a library within the branding guidelines of a wider organization?
Working with staff who do not always understand the significance of the service or product that you want to market can be difficult, but given a good relationship can also be rewarding. As LIS staff we are constantly at the 'user interface', so know our customers and know how they ask for things and what is likely to grab

their interest. This can sometimes appear to be too detailed for a central team, who may prefer to give headline messages that aim to build brand recognition rather than inform on a detailed or contextual level. For this reason, word of mouth through presentations works better than developing marketing brochures where you are balancing the needs of several stakeholder interests. Speaking direct to our member audiences allows us to control the message.

We have had some experience of marketing staff re-writing copy in what they regard as house style. On occasions this has altered the meaning of the message and we have had to work towards a compromise to balance medium, message and style. We found the marketing professionals to be mainly receptive to this and we've been able to arrive at a successful conclusion.

Some other challenges include:

- meeting our own budget timelines because of having to build in the time to negotiate on brand approvals
- delays caused by repetitive re-approval for amendments
- use of outside agencies builds in additional layers and can complicate and delay
- getting an individuality and recognized personality for the LIS within a unified brand that promotes one organization.

And how have you met these challenges? What worked for you that you feel other libraries could apply to their own situations?

1 Welcome the branding people into your environment and meet them there, not least in order to expose them to the environment.
2 It is crucial to get familiar with every aspect of the branding guidelines so that you can avoid mistakes that will lose credibility. Equally important is to develop good relationships with the marketing and branding teams. It helps if you use their vocabulary.
3 Demonstrating that we had ideas and flair and that we are progressive helped – you need to shatter preconceptions. After one successful discussion about images and taglines, a marketing colleague who had previously been a little protective of territory remarked that we should attend their team brainstorms. Show initiative, keep it snappy.
4 Knowing when to give way – when marketing staff want to change something, if it is not substantive to the message, agree pleasantly, even if you prefer your own version. It means that when you do need to dig your heels in, you have some credit for not always seeming to disagree with their

proposals. However, think clever; be prepared to negotiate; remember flexibility is not 'giving in', it's achieving your main goals and accommodating the rest (you need to be able to recognize the point at which this has been reached so that you don't start to undermine what's been achieved so far); don't be defensive or aggressive: you have a service and a product to be proud of.

5 Speaking to our members directly. In the final quarter of the past two years I e-mailed every Regional and District Society office and offered to speak at one of their events or meetings (an 18-month programme was the result and further requests are still being made for 2012 events). Not only did this provide a direct opportunity to give key messages – 'We are happy to come to you; we are friendly and knowledgeable; we know what sort of information needs you have' – it gained us high profile within the ICAEW. The CEO has been at a meeting in one of the regions and chartered accountants have remarked to him 'we had a really great talk from the Head of Library Services last month, caused a lot of interest, seems like a really great service', etc. In turn, this gets brownie points for the CEO for making these services available.

I personally feel that bravery is a quality often lacking in our industry. I imagine it is even harder to be brave in your marketing when trying to do so within a wider organization's branding guidelines – do you have any feelings on getting the balance right between caution and being a bit more dynamic in promoting our services?

I have always followed the general rule that it is easier to obtain forgiveness than to get permission. I think that on the whole, providing you are able to explain what you want to do and use the language marketing people use, you can get away with bold ideas. This year we have designed two 'pull-up' banners for exhibitions and events. We chose very bold images (but used ICAEW image bank so there was no question of their being inappropriate for the brand) with equally striking messaging. And there's another type of bravery – daring to put forward suggestions that may be scoffed at. By putting them in the discussion arena a far-fetched idea might be developed into an original marketing tool.

I was delighted to see that in the 'Benefits of membership' section of the Chartered Institute's website, the library service is listed first! Do you have any advice on how librarians might convince their own parent organizations of their value?

Consider what is of monetary or strategic interest to your organization and its decision-makers and latch onto that as context: at ICAEW members pay an annual fee to continue to call themselves Chartered Accountants and use their post-nominals. Obviously it is in their interest to feel they are getting value for their subscription; it is in the ICAEW's interest to have something tangible they can say they provide from fee income.

Finally, I'm very interested in the use of online tools in marketing corporate libraries. You have to fit in with the corporate ethos, but at the same time social media does need to be informal and fairly colloquial to work successfully – how do you balance that (or plan to)?
In the early days of our online presence we actively marketed our content by soliciting links and participated in online discussion forums to promote relevant resources. However, we found that this was less effective than focusing on our online content to make sure it was well written and of good quality – ensuring that it would be well indexed and ranked by search engines (i.e. effective SEO).

A significant percentage of our online promotion today is focused on collaborating with internal stakeholders – helping and encouraging them to leverage our resources for web projects and initiatives that are intended to engage our members/students and their other target audiences.

At the moment, our social media strategy is focused on embedding library marketing into existing corporate social media streams. We collaborate regularly with ICAEW's marketing and digital communications departments to promote library services and content in blogs, webinars and e-mail newsletters. As for juggling the more colloquial tone of social media within a corporate environment, we're lucky that this isn't an issue for us – the benefit of working within such a large corporate organization is that there's already a well informed communications policy dealing with web and social media.

More information and further reading on internal marketing can be found at **www.librarymarketingtoolkit.com/p/internal-marketing.html**.

CHAPTER 10
Library advocacy as marketing

At first glance internal marketing and library advocacy are opposites, with one being very inward-facing and the other very outward-facing – but in fact the two are closely linked. They both involve proving the library's value to people who really matter. I firmly believe that we are *all* library advocates now. It is not something any information professional can afford to abstain from; in fact to abstain is to contribute to the problem.

Marketing and advocacy have a close link. They are both about the promotion of libraries and library services. The point of this brief chapter is to explore how library advocacy per se can be used as a marketing opportunity for *your specific library*. It will also introduce 'the echo chamber problem' – an issue which afflicts all libraries but one which can be addressed relatively easily with a slight shift in mindset – and features a case study from Elizabeth Elford, Head of Advocacy at the British Library.

National campaigns and local marketing

In a time of closures and cuts, national library advocacy campaigns are increasingly frequent. They are of course an entirely worthwhile thing to be part of in their own right, but it's also possible to glean direct, regional benefit for your library even from a national campaign about libraries in general.

Jan Richards co-ordinated the '@ your library' campaign in New South Wales, Australia. He provides a full case study all about this online (see the further reading for this chapter on the website) but here are some pertinent quotes about the local value libraries derived from it:

> The *@ your library* campaign was designed to be delivered at a local level but to gain strength from the same story being told from many different viewpoints/places. So while libraries used their traditional channels to promote

the initiative it was often picked up at a regional level because of the 'noise' of the message. There was also the opportunity to use this strength in selling the story to the major news agencies.

In many ways the major impact of the campaign was largely local, despite its NSW-wide rollout. What it did achieve, however, was dispelling some myths about public libraries. The sleek, professional look of the campaign material and the website; the collection of hard evaluative data; and the inclusiveness of the rollout definitely impacted on how libraries were regarded by many of their stakeholders, in particular their funding bodies, the local councils. A number of libraries were able to successfully exploit this; the professional media releases and images ensured extensive local coverage; the striking design work helped repositioned libraries as vibrant, modern spaces; and the sharing of ideas provided a collaborative, collegiate environment which opened up opportunities for future projects between libraries and other community partners.

Promoting your library in response to criticism of libraries in general

National criticism of libraries per se is actually a great opportunity to promote your library in particular. Publications like *Times Higher Education* and *Higher Education Chronicle* seem to carry derogatory articles about the modern academic library on an annual basis, perpetuating the usual myths about how 'libraries are getting rid of all the books to make space for bean-bags' and so on. A well argued response piece or letter from an academic library explaining just how fabulous their modern library is will help perceptions of libraries generally but specifically promote that library too. When academic staff read this they may update their opinions about your institution.

The same principle applies to misguided opinion pieces about public libraries in national newspapers. Respond in the same publication (or in the Comments section online), ensuring the same audience sees the positive message about libraries as saw the negative, and extol the virtues of *your* library. Even better, invite the author to see your library for themselves and turn the whole thing into some brilliant PR. In the UK, comedian, author and broadcaster Frank Skinner wrote an article for *The Times* entitled 'Sorry, the demise of libraries is well overdue' (2010a) in which he argued that most public libraries should be closed and that this would be a positive step. Then he was invited (by a hand-written letter, which caught his attention unlike the stream of digital feedback newspaper articles receive, which most authors appear to tune out from completely) to visit Church Street Library, London, in person – in order to show him the error of his ways. To his credit he went, and then wrote a very honest follow-up, also in *The Times*, entitled 'Why I'm on a new page with libraries: it was my ideas about libraries which were dog-eared, not the places themselves' (Skinner, 2010b). Overall, thanks to the person who invited him to the library, the piece ended up causing more positive publicity then if he'd never talked about libraries at all, and resulted in some fantastic PR for one library in particular.

Advocacy, promotion and positive messages

Elizabeth Elford provides the case study for this chapter, and she occupies an unusual role in the library advocacy effort. As well as being a marketing expert in her own right, Elizabeth is Public Libraries Advocacy Manager for the Society of Chief Librarians (SCL) in the UK, made up of every senior librarian/head of library service in England, Wales and Northern Ireland. (Be sure to have a look at their statistics page, filled with powerful figures demonstrating the use and importance of libraries: www.goscl.com/media/public-libraries.) In addition to this she is Head of Advocacy at the British Library, as the BL is keen to support work in this area: she has her office on their premises, and access to all their communications resources. Here she discusses many aspects of advocacy and marketing.

Case study 23: Advocacy and library marketing | Elizabeth Elford

How do we get the balance right between the local and national profile of our libraries? Presumably there are different messages that we should be promoting to different stakeholders.

I feel strongly that every single library authority needs a communications strategy for its libraries. This should complement the local authority's overarching communications strategy. At every opportunity (every local authority publication, event, etc.) libraries should be looking to pitch their own messages.

Of course, there are many different stakeholders to consider and messages will differ locally and nationally. Locally, libraries need to promote themselves to elected members, the public, the media and customers. Also very important is promoting library work to other local authority departments. Libraries should be looking to each and every person working in a local authority as a potential cheerleader for libraries. (Excuse the Americanism, but it is true. Word of mouth is vital.)

On a national level, libraries can promote their services and stories to their MPs, who need to be better informed about libraries. There are many organizations working at a national level on library advocacy, in some form or another. The Society of Chief Librarians, CILIP, The Reading Agency, just to name a few.

Back to stakeholders. Libraries should have a bank of key messages in their communications strategy, and some will resonate more with certain stakeholders than others. It is important to find out where the motivations and interests of stakeholders lie, and this can be done simply by following what they say in the media, the white papers and research produced, or the best method, by meeting with them to gauge interest and knowledge.

Can you give us some tips for library advocacy in general which can benefit our own libraries specifically?
Start with a simple and clear communications strategy. If you have one that you drafted and then never looked at, it probably needs refreshing. I recommend beginning this with a brainstorm – four to six people around a table for three hours in the morning to flesh out goals, messages and tactics. Don't just get your own library staff involved – ask your elected members. Ask someone from the authority's communications team. Ask a customer to participate. This is an opportunity to build your squad of cheerleaders.

Go back to basics with your key messages and choose a few very powerful ones that you want to promote.

Make sure you have a method for collecting personal case studies about how libraries are helping people to change their lives and achieve their potential. Ask customers if you can use their quotes and stories. Be bold. The Get It Loud in Libraries initiative has been very controversial yet also written about everywhere. I just read an article in a New York newspaper about it. Be bold.

When it comes to stakeholders, give them information that they can use to make themselves look good. That's how it works – let them shine, make sure they are properly briefed, and they can become strong advocates for you.

Librarians can reach all the usual channels with our advocacy efforts, but it's important to try and reach new audiences too. To do that we need other people. Any tips on building relationships with third parties who can spread our message beyond the echo chamber?

Every person you meet is a potential advocate. Or a potential naysayer, depending on the kind of experience you give them. So treat everyone as such. Stay positive, give people a good experience and they will tell ten friends. Here is where you make the list, in your communications brainstorm, of your audiences and figure out how you reach them with your key messages. Local radio, local newspapers, social media sites. Use them all.

Libraries, are, famously, 'free'. This should be an asset, but people take it for granted and in a lot of cases people value things less if they pay less for them. How can we position libraries as something which people feel they ought to be paying for, so that the 'freeness' is once again a major selling point?
This is a difficult question. Libraries need to make sure their spaces are beautiful and welcoming. If the sofa in the reading section is stained and grotty, buy a cover. Or a new sofa. The space is very important. As is the stock. It is fine for things to look used, but lovingly used, not trashed. I think every library could stand to take a hard look at itself through the eyes of a first-time customer and clear away the cobwebs. I have been in libraries that had little to no budget for renovation but were lovingly cared for and it showed. Also, I've visited libraries which had bigger budgets but were cluttered, or the staff was unkempt and rude, or the sofa was stained. People want to spend time in nice places.

And yes, when you walk into a library you should feel like it would be something worth paying for. Actually we are paying. We are all paying. I moved here from Russia, where I lived for eight years, and the tax rate there is 13%, incredibly low. And there aren't any nice libraries to sit and read or go online in. Before that I was in my home country, in America, where libraries have much more local philanthropic investment in them. And corporate investment.

I feel that is a path that libraries need to consider. Developing ties with businesses and corporations and philanthropists. There is much untapped opportunity in the UK to improve libraries through corporate and individual philanthropy. And so what if that means part of the library will be branded? I think people need to get over that and accept that if the bottom line is improving a library service, that is what matters most.

But the most important thing is pride. People who work in libraries should be proud of them. Customers should be proud of them. Local councillors should be proud. Your MP should be proud and talking about the library in Westminster and every else they visit. The local newspaper should be proud.

The library media narrative

Central to our efforts to market libraries as a whole is the need to position ourselves within the 'library media narrative', a phrase first coined by Ian Clark (2010). That is to say, how the story of libraries is told in the public eye, and by whom. At the moment this narrative is being dictated to and for us by others: third parties who might not have libraries' best interests at heart.

As Elizabeth Elford states:

> Public libraries as we know them won't survive unless we get positive stories out about the work that they do. If we are consistently fed only negative stories via the media, public confidence will go down, people will use libraries even less than they do now, and funding will decrease. It surprises and amazes me at how much is going on in libraries that is virtually unheard of outside of the library world. Libraries are going about their daily business of inspiring people but yet most of them are keeping mum about it. Because they assume everyone knows. They don't!

Often the reason our voice isn't heard is that we are too busy talking only to each other, within the 'echo chamber' of the profession, rather than to those external figures whose views we might wish to influence. The echo chamber effect refers to any situation in which information, ideas or beliefs are amplified or reinforced by transmission inside an 'enclosed' space. My presenting partner Laura Woods and I have adapted to this to apply to the way in which we too often preach to the converted on the value of libraries. We discuss how important or excellent our libraries are with like-minded peers who already share this view, and they echo our opinions back at us; meanwhile those who are hostile to libraries (or indifferent to them) don't hear a word from us. Our opinions stay within the chamber (the enclosed space) of the library community, and just echo about without ever reaching an external audience or being challenged by a dissenting voice.

A typical example of the echo chamber phenomenon as a problem in our profession occurs when libraries or librarians are criticized from outside the industry, for instance by a national newspaper or television programme. The first reaction of many librarians is to find another librarian and indignantly discuss how unfair the coverage was – but of course this doesn't serve much of a purpose, except letting off steam. Occasionally the librarian will take this a stage further and write an article for a library publication about how wrong the newspaper/television was, which will only be read by other librarians.

Great for firing up the profession, but not enough on its own – we have to reach beyond our own walls and defend libraries publicly.

The echo chamber problem is one that you can begin to address as soon as you become aware of its existence. Our role is to assert some control of the narrative with louder voices, and ensure we are telling our own story – not least by writing for publications our patrons read, and appearing in the broadcast media they watch and listen to, and speaking at events our patrons go to. Aim high: market your library on a national or international scale. The main message is this: if you are going to take the time to defend or espouse the value of libraries, try and do it in such a way that it reaches new audiences – and if you can highlight the value of libraries in general by talking up your library in particular, so much the better.

Trojan horse advocacy

Stealth advertising (also known as 'undercover marketing') is the process of advertising a product or brand without the consumer knowing it is happening. The most common example is product placement on television or in films – no one is overtly saying 'Drink product X!' but the attractive characters are seen with conspicuously placed cans of product X all the time. This is complicated, expensive, and in many people's view, unethical – as such, it isn't something libraries are likely to attempt soon. Trojan horse advocacy (or, to adapt the previous phrase, stealth *advocizing*), however, is its library-related cousin, and is much less morally dubious and much more easily achievable.

As one would expect from the name, this is the process of disguising library marketing and advocacy in a distracting or otherwise beguiling outer casing in order to gain entry to otherwise inaccessible places. The kind of people who think they already know what libraries do are not going to read a pamphlet called 'This is what libraries do' – they will likely dismiss it as unnecessary. Therefore, the only way to reach them is to dress the same information up in such an attractive way that they're drawn to the medium rather than the content – they then ingest the content at the same time.

My own attempt at stealth advocizing involved something as simple as a slide deck. Entitled 'Want to work in libraries? Here are 10 things you need to know', it purported to be aimed at prospective library professionals, outlining the realities of the job. Indeed, it did serve this purpose – but my primary motivation was to let people know the realities of the modern library: the fast-paced, technologically literate environment in which we worked. The idea was to challenge assumptions and update people on the services we really offer in the 21st century. I made the slide deck as attractive as possible in the hope that it might reach new audiences that way – people interested in a well made presentation, rather than libraries per se – and then put it on Slideshare.net, the presentation sharing website mentioned in the *Marketing with new technologies* chapter. The result was better than I'd dared hope – it became a featured presentation on both the main site and the 'Education' section, and it was 'hot' (which is to say most-often shared online during a given period of time) on Twitter, Facebook and LinkedIn. Because of all this, it was seen by around 40,000 people, embedded in over 100 websites across the world, and linked to in an article from the *Guardian* website – clearly, not all those viewers were already librarians, so hopefully some attitudes shifted as a result.

The aim with Trojan horse advocacy, then, must be to engage an audience who otherwise would not be interested in the library. If there are library staff with exceptional talents in the areas of design, film-making or any other area of the arts, this type of promotion for your specific library may be an avenue worth exploring.

For more information about the echo-chamber problem, links, and further resources (including the full Jan Richards case study mentioned earlier), see this chapter's web page: **www.librarymarketingtoolkit.com/p/advocacy-as-marketing.html**.

CHAPTER 11

Marketing special collections and archives

Introduction

Special collections and archives come with their own set of marketing challenges and techniques. I'm going to risk the wrath of both communities by stating that although special collections and archives are often distinct areas, there are many similarities in the way they are marketed. Certainly it is the case that some ideas and methods can apply to both and it is these on which we'll be focusing in this chapter.

Although this chapter concentrates on the specific challenges of these related sectors, it's worth making clear that many of the ideas apply in marketing libraries more broadly (tying in your promotional activity with the wider cultural landscape, for example) and, conversely, most of the other techniques described in this book still very much apply in special collections and archives, too. In particular, the need for a strategic approach is still relevant, and using social media to promote archives can be very effective: old source material and new technologies are surprisingly comfortable bedfellows. Every marketing channel should be exploited, and every market considered, as Caroline Kimbell of The National Archives (TNA) says:

> Even under the constraints of a marketing freeze, TNA has managed to keep its public profile high and its media presence a constant. This isn't just because we have great stories to tell from the documents and people who know them, but because we've been creative in how we use all the free tools and services available to reach new and existing audiences, and borne in mind the broad range of user groups who use and interact with our collections – from schoolchildren and academic researchers to journalists, authors, family historians and information management professionals.

There are four case studies here. Caroline Kimbell focuses on digitization and the 'halo effect'. Then Alison Cullingford at Bradford University Library talks us through some modern ways of marketing ancient materials, with the 100 Objects campaign. Ben Showers of JISC focuses on harnessing the power of crowds, and the marketing benefits this can bring. To kick the chapter off, we have the first case study – expert advice on marketing archives from Lisa Jeskins. Lisa is in charge of 'Promotion and Outreach: Library and Archival Services' for Mimas, which hosts a number of the UK's research information assets and builds applications to help people use them. She gives a brief list of tips for marketing archives, and talks about many aspects of the process which feature later on in this chapter.

Case study 24: Five top tips for marketing an archive service | Lisa Jeskins

Marketing an archive service can be tough. As an archivist or special collections librarian, you could be working solo, with little or no budget for marketing. However, you have access to a wealth of treasures located in your archive which you could and should shout about. Marketing strategies need to be based upon your organization's strategy or vision for the future. Doing this will not only support your organization in achieving its goals, it will provide you with a clear purpose and help to secure management support.

1 Objective setting and evaluation

When planning your marketing strategy make sure that your objectives are SMART (Specific, Measurable, Achievable, Relevant and Timely). Ensuring objectives are measurable allows you to evaluate your efforts and ascertain if your plan has been a success. This helps you to review your current work and to plan for the future! A marketing plan should be reviewed continuously.

2 Key audiences

It is essential to work out who your audience is. Who are you trying to reach? And what are you trying to achieve by talking to them? You can have different key messages for different audiences but you need to do some research into who uses your services and who might use them (if only they knew about them). It is worthwhile using marketing tools such as segmentation to think about your audiences. I believe if you work out who you are talking to, it is easier to work out what to say.

3 Key messages

Are there fundamental messages about your archive or repository that users should know? What are your compelling stories? When thinking about what you want to communicate to your users, consider the following: what are your stories? What are you doing that's clever and what are you doing that's interesting? Think about what catches your eye. Is it that you have a new archival management system? Well, possibly, if one of your objectives is to raise awareness amongst other archivists and you can engage them by blogging about the trials and tribulations of installing a new system. However, do your users/visitors care? It's unlikely. Think more about what you have in your collections and how you can exploit them. Can you link messages and campaigns to television programmes such as *Who Do You Think You Are?* Are there any national programmes, themes or anniversaries you can use? Are you having any exhibitions to coincide with anything of this nature? – e.g. with the Olympics, Diamond Jubilee or the anniversary of a notable individual? Also think about your objectives, what do you want your audience to do, once they have read/received your message? Or what do you want them to do differently? Are you simply raising awareness or do you want them to visit? Go to the website? Follow you on Twitter?

4 Key channels

Your channels for communication may well depend on your budget. If you have one. If you do, then can you pay to advertise? You could use the local media (newspapers/radio) to advertise an open day or exhibition. However, if, as has been the case for many public sector organizations, there have been budget cuts in this area, you might want to think of using other free channels of communication, such as your website, e-mail, creating a blog, setting up a Twitter account or a Facebook page. If you are going to try social media then this might be a great low-budget way of engaging with your target audience. These are channels that need updating regularly, so you will need to make sure you have the resources (time/staff) to do so. Twitter accounts and Facebook pages only really work when organizations really engage with them and your followers (or people who 'like' your page) believe you are providing them with a value-added service, not just using the account to broadcast.

5 Getting online

If you haven't already, then you need to start thinking about creating a website and getting your descriptions online. Even if you only have the resource to create collection-level descriptions, having them online allows users to have some point of entry in to your collections. It also means that your 'user group' increases. Now you're not only talking to physical visitors but to a new wave of online users. These users could increase your reading room statistics through their initial use of your website. Once your descriptions are online then you can also put them into an online aggregation such as Aim25 or the Archives Hub. This will help to raise your profile, particularly if you don't have your own online catalogue. All of these things will help users to find you when they search Google. Get yourself out there (and by out there I mean online!). Think outside the box, innovate, be where your users are and most of all, have fun! If you're having fun and are enthused by something then this will communicate itself to your users.

Armed with this basic framework, we can now go on to look at specific areas of marketing.

Access, access, access: marketing digital collections

In the past, there has been an idea that librarians are the gatekeepers of knowledge – the guardians of all that is valuable. Thanks to the internet's democratization of information, those gates are now wide open and in most cases our role has changed to that of Sherpa, helping people navigate the terrain beyond. In special collections and archives, however, something of the old hierarchy still exists. It is difficult for people to access these rather elite-seeming areas of the library, so we have to fight to overturn the perception that the information they contain is unobtainable. It is easy to focus on the monetary value of our special collections, but their real value (in terms of demonstrating the ongoing importance of the library) is in their *use*. People must feel they can use these materials as far as is practically possible. There are issues with the over-use of old and fragile original material, so this section will focus on marketing the digital. Increasingly, investment from external funding is being poured into digitizing archives and special collections.

Anyone who has ever been involved with digitization will know there is a digital lifecycle. There are various models for this, but essentially what it boils down to is planning your digitization, capturing your digital object, storing your digital object, and sharing your digital object. It is a bizarre truth that this last stage of the process – which is often primarily what the other three are *for* – is often overlooked, or is the least considered. But actually we have a duty to make our collections available to people, and that means more than just putting the digitized items online somewhere; it means making people aware of where they are and how then can use them. If you look at the money spent on marketing access to digital collections versus the money spent on actually digitizing them, you begin to see just how out of kilter our priorities are here.

In a case study appearing in *ALISS Quarterly*, Harvard's Christine McCarthy Madsen (2009) describes a digitization project in which 2% of the budget was spent on marketing. This seems like a tiny proportion, but nevertheless for the next project they were pressured to spend less on promotion and outreach, in order to digitize more material. The result was that the second digitized collection received *less than half* the web traffic of the first; in short, far fewer people knew about it, so far fewer people used it. Was it worth that massive drop in actual *use* just to be able to put more items online? I would argue not. Promotion of digital collections shouldn't be an afterthought; it should be embedded in the whole process.

Here are some principles for marketing the digital:

1 Metadata is essential to enable discoverability, but don't prioritize creating the perfect record over actually getting items online for the viewing public. Perfection can be, in this case, something of a red herring.
2 In exhibitions and displays, market the digital alongside the analogue. Use display screens to show relevant digitization above the physical original or, better still, touch-screen tablets that allow users to interact with the material in some way.
3 Highlight new content via virtual exhibitions, promoted online and grouped by some kind of theme (for example, World War II, or 12th-Century Illuminated Manuscripts). If you mount different exhibitions each month or each season, it gives visitors a reason to keep coming back.
4 Try to make online exhibitions immediately accessible to the viewer – rather than their having to download viewing software or indeed the content itself. Remember, it doesn't just have to be images and explanatory text: videos and audio recordings can enrich the experience.
5 Licensing images for commercial use can be a great revenue stream for the library, but consider giving some material away for free at first, to help build reputation.

6 Record throughput and record use. When a funding opportunity arises, you will have figures to hand that will prove your institution's ability to engage people with special collections and archives.

The British Library make their online materials brilliantly accessible, through their online galleries (see www.bl.uk/onlinegallery). Their budgets will be in excess of what most other libraries can afford, but the way in which they creatively display their online material is still a great example from which much can be learned. Their Sacred Contexts online gallery, for example, at www.bl.uk/sacred, offers video, audio and other interactive options to bring the digitized texts to life. One of the features at the time of writing is 'Curator's Choice', in which the BL's experts discuss six important texts – you can listen online, and there are written transcripts provided. This would be relatively easy and inexpensive to reproduce for any special collections or archive – see Chapter 7 for information about creating podcasts.

An excellent argument for digitization is that it protects the physical originals. Every time an ancient manuscript is handled, it decays somewhat – the same even applies to audio-visual materials recorded on modern magnetic tape such as VHS videos. Reduce the handling and you will preserve the resource. The end result of digitization is increased usability and discoverability; more people are able to get to what you have. The National Archives (TNA) discovered this to be the case to such an extent that digitization has acted as a form of marketing by association for their physical collections, increasing awareness, interest and engagement from the public. As a business model, 'the halo effect' describes the situation when one item is so popular that it positively influences the entire brand of which it is a part – a notable recent example being the iPod and its effect on Apple's brand. TNA have found that their digitized collections have had a halo effect on their entire organization; Caroline Kimbell, their Head of Licensing, describes this phenomenon, and other key aspects of their marketing strategy.

Case study 25: Digitization and the halo effect at TNA | Caroline Kimbell

I understand that when you digitize a collection, physical consultation of that collection goes down but physical consultation at the TNA overall goes up. Can you tell us about this and what causes it?

When we digitize a complete series of records, we stop productions of the paper originals. This reduction of wear and tear represents one of the main benefits of online access for us. However, the online audience is potentially global, and in any case, far larger than the visitor group to a physical reading room, so the number of people who become aware of your content once it's online is much higher than your physical audience. This is especially the case if the records are being actively marketed by a successful, international publisher such as Ancestry or Findmypast. The by-product of online exposure is therefore a large group of people who are now intrigued or attracted by what else the original archive has to offer, and who start to appear in the reading room wanting to read around the collection they have already seen. We call this the 'halo effect' and while it's perhaps counter-intuitive that putting material online produces more visitors in person, it's the inevitable result of scaling up public awareness of a collection. The popularity of *Who Do You Think You Are?* on TV has led to an upsurge in public curiosity about family history and archival sources, so the effects of the two together are impossible to separate. By far the biggest proportion of our usage is online. My own department is measured in terms of the ratio between onsite and online document usage, and the current ratio is well over 200:1, with over 130 million document downloads of our content in 2010.

Do you think marketing archives differs fundamentally from marketing libraries, and if so how?
This isn't my area of expertise, but I would say that libraries market themselves on their community role as meeting points, cyber-cafés and lifelong learning centres in addition to traditional educational and leisure use, whereas archives present and explain themselves more in terms of the uniqueness of their collections, and the importance not just of memory and accountability that the records represent, but of the totally individual stories that people can find there. The personal emotional impact of discovering an ancestor in the past, and the jolt of realizing that individuals are waiting to be rediscovered and perhaps exonerated or lauded for their role in the community, or nation, makes archives unique resources which offer a distinct experience from using published material in a library.

Are there specific tools or materials you've found to be particularly effective in marketing archives?
Because we have been working under a marketing freeze across the public sector for over a year now, marketing activity has to be zero cost, so we're using as many external partners to get our message across as possible, and increasing web usage

by such means as Flickr, a TNA Twitter feed, Facebook page and constant press and media coverage. On Flickr, most recently we mounted a complete collection of rare photographs from colonial Africa, *Africa Through a Lens,* and asked people to tag people, places or events they recognized. This was heavily used for the first few weeks when media coverage was in people's awareness, and has been taken up by embassies and consulates in Africa today who have been using them as outreach and engagement material. Our 'D-Day in real time' tweets last year were a huge success, and proved an immediate way to engage people in historical research in a vivid, immediate way.

Podcasts are another very low-cost way of reaching far bigger audiences for our talks and conference papers than the onsite events could ever reach, and downloads of our weekly public talks usually run into the thousands.

How much do you focus your marketing on specific collections or events, as opposed to TNA generally?
We maintain an events and anniversaries calendar for up to four years ahead, and for major events such as the World War I centenary from 2014, we will plan and invest in such events as conferences, seminars, exhibitions (online and in the museum) and collaborative projects with other archives and museums. However, our media support for more general activity such as our regular new year, UFO and MI5 file releases run throughout the year, and whenever we have a new feature or content launch online, such as the new catalogue known as 'Discovery' launched in 2011, we will try to gather as much publicity as possible within the funding constraints. We have used techniques like Google ad-words when budget was available to boost our web profile, but we generally rely on our existing, very low-cost e-Newsletter to reach a worldwide audience when we need to communicate about new online content, new services or site features.

What can smaller-scale archives learn about marketing from a huge national organization such as TNA? Are there any lessons which apply equally to both?
Use all the free channels that are available! Social media is largely free and can have a real role to play in raising profile and generating conversations and interest in your collection. Time and resource devoted to communications is a vital investment in keeping not just your users but your funders aware of the importance of your organization and your collections.

TNA licenses commercial images – what is the key to utilizing this practice as a revenue stream successfully?

Apart from having compelling content which commercial publishers can sell, the biggest key is in having people in the archive who understand and can work with private partners. We are big enough to have a small team dedicated to licensing, and our backgrounds are in commercial publishing, project management and legal drafting. However, TNA offers advisory services and template agreements to all archives and is, at the time of writing, leading the bidding and evaluation process for a national consortium of over 100 local archives and records offices to allow and encourage them to get started in commercial digitization.

Is there one essential piece of advice which you'd like to share with other institutions marketing archive materials?
The crucial element for successful partnership with commercial publishers, especially in the family history field (less so for academic publishers) is to encourage and support competition. No contracts should ever offer exclusive rights: contracts for public records cannot legally offer exclusivity, but non-exclusivity is always highly recommended. If an archive were ever to find itself dealing with a monopoly supplier the ability to negotiate terms would be severely limited, so whenever an archive needs to work with the private sector – in order not just to raise revenue and bring in investment in scanning and transcription of its records but also to raise its profile and market itself – the key is competition.

Genealogy

Genealogy – the study of family history and lineage – is in a boom phase, having been so easily enabled via the internet, and thanks to the popularity of television shows on the subject such as *Who Do You Think You Are?* It is now one of the most popular forms of self-directed learning, and special collections and archives still often hold key information about families which isn't yet available elsewhere.

As well as promoting the library as a source of records and documents (it's easy to imagine the quick-win opportunities of having a poster featuring a famous family tree, ending with 'YOU?' at the bottom), the area of genealogy is a great opportunity to promote two library services at once. Many public libraries and archives run an 'Introduction to genealogy' class one week, offering a précis of how to get started and how to navigate the various commercial sites that allow you to trace your ancestry, and then an

'Introduction to finding archive material' as a follow-up, in which the participants take their new searching abilities into your physical archive to try and find more information about their forebears.

Tailoring your marketing to fit the cultural landscape

A great opportunity for marketing archives and special collections is to tie in your promotional activities wherever possible with what is going on in the wider cultural landscape. The public and your users will already understand the context, allowing you to concentrate solely on the content you are promoting. Anniversaries, for example those marking the end of wars or the signing of famous treaties, afford natural opportunities to tie in the relevant materials you have in this area with the wider public consciousness. More flimsy premisses can be valuable too: for example, an online 'Advent Calendar' campaign which features a blog post with different beautiful images for the first 24 days of December is a nice way to engage with the community and get wider awareness for the treasures in your collection.

Arts programmes on television and radio which are attracting national press coverage are a particularly good source of inspiration for exhibitions. Alison Cullingford, Special Collections Librarian at the University of Bradford, launched her own 100 Objects project in light of the BBC Radio 4 series, The History of the World in 100 Objects, in conjunction with the British Museum. She takes us through the campaign here.

Case study 26: The 100 Objects project | Alison Cullingford

The 100 Objects online exhibition of special collections at the University of Bradford is an example of a low-cost innovative project which uses social media to reach wider audiences. It began with my concern that so much interesting information, images and ideas about special collections are locked up in the minds of staff or on local servers. I wanted to transform them into some kind of online exhibition to help promote the collections and encourage virtual visits. It was difficult to see how we could do this with the conventional website. I had some success using the special collections blog, which gets many hits, but I felt that a stronger identity or brand was needed to bundle the stories together and separate them from our other news and reflections.

The revelation came on a day when in two separate meetings three or four different people were raving about the British Museum's 100 Objects series. It occurred to me that audiences who might be interested in special collections would already know about the British Museum's project and that doing something similar for our own collections would enable us to piggy-back on that knowledge. After a lot of thought and planning, I came up with a way of using the 100 Objects concept that worked for our situation and our audiences.

Unlike the British Museum, our objects don't tell one story. I decided that there was no one story that needed 100 objects to tell it; instead, each object is its own story, though they do of course link and overlap. This approach allows us to capture the diversity of subjects and people in special collections, and to appeal to different audiences via different objects. The exhibition centres on a Wordpress blog, where every week a new object is introduced, in about 300 words, with plenty of images, sometimes video. Each object is also added to our Facebook page and Flickr site and heavily promoted via the @100objectsbrad Twitter account and other media, including the University's staff briefing and library newsletter. The tone is more informal and personal than our conventional web, but much less chatty and opinionated than a personal blog. Note that I tend to call the project an exhibition rather than a blog, mainly because blog is a word that can turn off those who are not interested in social media, and also because this project is much more than just a blog.

I have been delighted with the response to the exhibition. It has gained a great deal of attention in-house and externally and the interest continues to build. The way it engaged University colleagues, especially senior management and marketing and development staff, has been particularly gratifying. The project was awarded Archives Pacesetter status by the Archives and Records Association in 2011.

100 Objects works because it was designed around audience interests and what was feasible with our resources. There are several pointers here for other libraries to consider in their marketing.

1 Borrow existing strong brands and ideas that are meaningful to your audience (obviously taking rights, etc. into account). This means you don't have to get over the hurdle of explaining your project.
2 Use ideas where it doesn't matter if someone else does something similar. Plenty of museums and organizations are offering variants on this theme. That doesn't matter, indeed we all help cross-promote each other.
3 Think about timescale. Events and other one-offs can be difficult to promote because there is only one chance to grab people's attention and engage

them. I see this project as water wearing away stone, gradually entering people's minds over the two years.

4 Build on what you have. The project uses existing skills and knowledge of the staff and repackages existing writing and images in more engaging and accessible ways.

5 Build in flexibility to respond to staffing issues or other new technology and possibilities. With 100 Objects, if a new platform emerges or a chance to publish or exhibit in physical form, the curation, writing and image capture has already been done. The project work (with the exception of digitizing physical objects) can be done at home or on the move and in the reading room while supervising readers. The platforms we use allow us to schedule posts and tweets well in advance.

6 Be aware of risk. The project is managed using formal project techniques, in particular assessing possible risks and taking action to limit or avoid them. I would suggest that anyone embarking on something on a similar scale think about staffing and technology risks and ensure the project can cope.

7 Think open source and free. Other than staff time, and a few social media upgrades, the project does not need extra expenditure because we use free stuff.

8 Don't bite off more than you can chew, but it is good to push yourself a little. Sometimes it can be hard getting the post done every week, but the commitment means it happens. I decided not to write the objects far in advance because I wanted to keep things fresh, but I know other projects will prefer to do it differently. I have built in the odd gap for annual leave or other commitments.

You can view the project at http://100objectsbradford.wordpress.com.

Mounting and promoting a more traditional exhibition

There is much focus in this chapter on the digital, but of course traditional marketing techniques still have value when used well. One such is the physical display or exhibition – a key factor in promoting special collections and archives. Alison Cullingford follows on from her full case study above with some expert advice in this area:

1 Exhibitions, like all marketing and promotion, should not be created for

the sake of having an exhibition, but to convey a message or story to particular audience(s). What are you trying to say and to whom?

2   Exhibitions, especially physical ones which require reproductions, captions, organizing space, etc., are far more time-consuming than most people imagine.

3   Any exhibition which includes some risk (e.g. it must be ready for a certain date, or involves work by external contractors) should be project-managed.

4   Stakeholders, senior management, etc. tend not to understand how time-consuming and expensive major exhibitions can be. Blockbuster exhibitions, of the sort seen at major museums, are months in the planning and can cost tens of thousands of pounds, and involve external designers etc. A solo librarian with many other duties would struggle to produce anything on such a scale. However, a small, cheaply created exhibition can be very effective.

5   Curation is the key. Who is in charge? Whose vision is it? To generalize wildly, individually curated exhibitions (or at least sections) tend to work better for visitors.

6   I find it helps to think of an exhibition as a different way of publishing. A small exhibition is like an article; a larger one like a monograph. This helps me to appreciate the scale and to think in terms of readers.

Learning from museums

Museums and special collections and archives are close cousins, and many of the marketing challenges and techniques are the same. One area in which libraries could learn a lot from museums, however, is marketing and tourism.

Museums are part of any region's tourist attractions and, where appropriate, there's no reason why special collections or archives shouldn't be too. If you have an amazing exhibition which captures the imagination, why not try and boost the number of visitors with people from outside the region, passing through? Museums achieve this in part through co-operating with local tourist boards, to get their names and locations into guides to the area and on promotional leaflets.

Continuing the theme, it can be worth sending out mailshots of leaflets for display, to local organizations who cater for tourists: hotels and bed and breakfast establishments, local museums and performance venues, and even coach operators. Good-quality paper is a must for this exercise, so that the paper doesn't fold or flop over when displayed on a rack.

Crowdsourcing

Put simply, crowdsourcing is the process of getting many to do the work normally only undertaken by a few specialists. Because it involves delegating work to a community, it is in itself a source of outreach and marketing – a rare chance to allow users to feel invested in their libraries and archives. Crowdsourcing can be used to collect materials (soliciting photographs from World War I for an online portal, for example) or even metadata (tagging photos for a historic map).

Ben Showers, a program manager with the Digital Infrastructure team at JISC (Joint Information Systems Committee), is an expert on crowdsourcing. Below he provides advice on setting up a crowdsourcing project and using it to market your library. For established crowdsourcing projects he provides a follow-up case study online, which covers promoting your crowdsourcing project, establishing and maintaining your online communities, and rights issues – see the link to the web page at the end of this chapter.

Case study 27: Harnessing the crowd – marketing your library with crowdsourcing | Ben Showers

An opportunity for libraries

Libraries are in an incredibly fortunate position. Their role at the centre of the communities they serve, whether academic, public, specialist or private, means that they have the enviable advantage of being truly socially engaged organizations. To help ensure this socially engaged role resonates far beyond a library's usual community; libraries need to think creatively about how they market and communicate their role and the services they provide. A number of libraries have recognized that crowdsourcing provides an opportunity to undertake large and complex tasks, as well as increase the online visibility of the library and engage users in an entirely new and more personalized way:

1 DigitalKoot (www.digitalkoot.fi/en/splash) from the National Library of Finland uses a game called Mole Hunt to crowdsource effort in correcting their newspaper indexes. Contributors can easily track their progress through the game dynamics of score and levels, and the top contributors find themselves on the front page of the website.
2 The Library of Congress has used Flickr to upload thousands of its historical photos: www.flickr.com/people/library_of_congress. The library used this

existing platform as a way to locate part of its collection in an online, social space people already inhabited. It also avoids the cost of building its own infrastructure and benefits from the tagging, sharing and social aspects of the Flickr site.

3 The National Library of Australia developed a project to correct and enhance the OCR (optical character recognition) text for its newspaper collection. Trove (http://trove.nla.gov.au) crowdsourced the effort of hundreds of thousands of people across the world to enhance its records and engaged users in a totally new way. The project has proven so popular that the library now uses the system to improve the text and metadata on books, photos, websites, maps and biographies.

The examples above highlight how individual libraries and library communities are taking advantage of crowdsourcing to extend their services and capture people's imaginations. The advantages of applying a crowdsourcing methodology to libraries, no matter how small the project/experiment is, can have a number of significant marketing benefits for the library involved – this short list is derived from Holley (2010):

- encouraging an unparalleled sense of engagement and ownership toward cultural heritage collections
- building a relationship between the library and users, including loyalty and trust
- demonstrating the value and importance of library services far beyond its original community
- giving the library and information providers first-hand evidence of users' needs and requirements, allowing the service to be improved or changed to serve the users' needs
- helping build new, virtual communities where users are brought together to share common experiences around the library space.

It is clear that crowdsourcing can have significant benefits for libraries in communicating and marketing the work they do. In order to support libraries in undertaking crowdsourcing projects it is useful to try and extract a number of key lessons that have surfaced from library crowdsourcing projects over the past few years.

Marketing libraries using crowdsourcing

Allow people to buy-in to your vision and aims. Before embarking on any kind of crowdsourcing experiment it is important for the library to identify exactly what its aims are for the project. These aims can then be translated into the project's goal: it is this that you are asking your participants to try and help you achieve.

Occupy (virtual) spaces that people already inhabit. Physical library buildings tend to be located in the heart of the communities they serve; this should be the aim of the library's online presence. Similarly, it is unlikely that users will come to you (unless you're the Library of Congress!). We're all habitual in our web travel, and unless you're the BBC or Facebook it's unlikely you're going to interrupt people's usual journeys across the web. Think about the popular spaces already on the web: YouTube; Tumblr; Twitter, and build a presence within them.

Rethink the distinction between the physical and the virtual. For example, why not allow library members (or, even better, anyone) to bring something related in from home and have it digitized and put online while they are in the library. This approach can help promote the project, involve a wider range of participants and establish early contributors and advocates for the project.

Promoting your crowdsourcing project

For any library looking to explore crowdsourcing it is important to understand how best to promote the project, and ensure that the work is able to gain those all important initial contributors. While crowdsourcing itself is a very powerful form of marketing and communications, it does require some effort to help spread the word about what you're trying to do, and get people's involvement. A number of useful lessons emerge from successful crowdsourcing projects that can help libraries effectively promote the project and recruit participants:

- Target specific groups and communities online: search and become members of groups focusing on topics relating to your content/focus, both on and offline.
- Use transitory events and celebrations: use events or celebrations on your theme/subject to promote your project.
- Don't forget the physical spaces: use libraries and other venues to hold events around the project; hold displays, advertise and, if possible, involve the local press.
- Utilize partners: could you involve partners that could help promote the work?

It is worth bearing in mind that the marketing of a crowdsource project is itself an extension of marketing the library and the resources it provides.

In conclusion, crowdsourcing is one of the potential tools that libraries have at their disposal for engaging new and existing users and communities. It is an extremely effective way for libraries to market their services and role in an increasingly complex and digital information environment. As part of a marketing strategy crowdsourcing allows libraries to make services meaningful to each individual, adapt to changing needs and expectations and demonstrate the value of what they do.

Top 5 tips for libraries planning crowdsourcing

- Make your challenge BIG! The closer to impossible it seems, the more people will want to help and be a part of it.
- Let users know how well they are doing, either collectively or individually: competition and achievement work.
- Make it easy to use, contribute and submit.
- Keep the site active: you need to do some work too. Developing communities that are active and evolving takes effort and work.
- Be open and assume contributors are correct. Adding lots of checks and barriers will only act to discourage activity and creativity – also it is very unlikely you will get any vandalism or misuse.

Marketing audiovisual materials

Many archives have audio and video materials of interest to the public. They can be marketed in just the same way as the digitization of paper materials. As digitization becomes more common these become more accessible, subject to various copyright considerations. Here are some tips for engaging the community when digitizing audiovisual materials:

1 You may need to track down the original participants in the recording in order to gain permission to digitize – as you have their details, send them a copy of the digitized version. In many cases it will be something they haven't seen in years, and rekindling their interest in it can act as a form of outreach to help start the process of publicizing the new collection via word of mouth.
2 If you are digitizing archives of cultural tradition, look out for societies

and organizations (still in existence) which celebrate those traditions. They may have a Facebook presence, which would be a fantastic avenue to promote the materials.

3 Create master copies of the best possible quality, but make sure distribution copies are usable first and foremost. If a video is of too high a quality it will be of too big a file size to work over a streaming server, for example.

4 Brand shareable content. It's very easy for people to share audio and video using social media, so the goal should be to ensure the content is identifiably yours even if someone is viewing it via a third-party site. Put audio or visual idents in at the start or end of the multimedia clips you share.

5 On a related note, if copyright allows, put some video on YouTube or Vimeo. Of course most of the digitized video will be in a digital repository or equivalent secure environment, which will allow for far greater quality. But YouTube allows shareability, and this will allow the material to reach audiences and, if the material is well branded, draw them back to your archive.

More resources on the subject of this chapter, including Alison Cullingford's five top tips for marketing special collections, can be found at **www.librarymarketingtoolkit.com/p/marketing-special-collections-and.html**.

A final word on marketing libraries

Imagine that libraries didn't exist, and were invented tomorrow. People would flock to them! The challenge we face is to convey to people what we really do, rather than what they think we do, and to tell them how we fit into their lives and can help them get from A to B a little better. Marketing is the dialogue between us and the rest of the world which ensures our existing users continue to come back, and our potential users sign up for a membership card. Not everyone will find the library useful – but if we reach all of those who do, we'll never have to worry about our future again.

The idea of this book is to give you a toolkit of marketing ideas that will inspire you to act in your own library. In my ideal scenario, you came into this believing that marketing the library was probably a good idea, you're leaving convinced that it is essential, but most importantly you feel you have the knowledge to take a marketing project forward and do it well. I imagine most people will have dipped into this rather than read it from cover to cover, so I won't summarize the previous couple of hundred pages here; I want to use this space to say 'marketing isn't so hard, so be bold and have some fun'. If you want to ask any questions about the things in this text, or you just want to talk to someone else who feels passionate about marketing libraries, you can find me on the book's Twitter account: @libmarketing.

The skill-sets of the modern information professional and the modern marketer aren't so far apart, when all is said and done. Being a librarian has always been about finding the right information, for the right people, at the right time. Marketing a library is really just promoting the right benefits of that information, to the right people, at the right time – taking the useful and necessary services we provide, and making those who need them aware of them.

Take action while this is all fresh in your mind, and do some real marketing. The first step will of course depend entirely on where your library is already – it could be anything from setting up a Twitter account or dipping your toe into the waters of social media to finally creating a formal marketing plan to draw together your promotional activities and actually measure the outcomes. It may only be small adjustment to what happens at your library already – for example, creating more than one offer for different marketing segments, rather than taking a one-size-fits-all approach – or continuing your existing promotion but measuring different aspects of its success to see what works and what doesn't. Once you start thinking like a marketer you'll find the mindset can be applied right across the library – from making signs and notices friendly and easy to understand to tweaking the title of the information literacy workshop you're running, so that it instantly conveys the reason people should go. Even just applying the maxim 'market the benefits, not the features' should yield instant results. It really isn't difficult and it really does work.

If you're feeling really brave, set yourself a target to attract a certain number of new users within a particular time period. Then start to think about where these new users will come from – will you attract more people from existing groups, or tap into entirely new ones? Take your library's current services to form the basis of an offer, and adapt it to suit each target group, then choose the right tools and the right messages to communicate with them. Measure your success, learn from your failure, and then do it all again better next time.

Good marketing results in libraries being used more, libraries being used better, libraries being valued more highly, and libraries proving to the people who matter that they should not become a target for cuts. The only way to predict the future of libraries is to dictate it ourselves.

Glossary of Web 2.0 tools and platforms

This Appendix acts as a companion piece and glossary for Chapter 6, 'Marketing with Social Media', for those not entirely *au fait* with the tools being discussed.

Web 2.0

You won't find a specific part of the internet called Web 2.0 (which when said aloud is commonly shortened to 'web two'): the term refers to web applications which feature interactivity, user-generated content, interoperability and user collaboration. It is not, despite what the nomenclature implies, a replacement or new version of the plain old world wide web – it is merely an aspect of it. There are still plenty of important and successful websites that allow users to consume the content provided passively, without any kind of action on their part; Web 2.0 sites tend to involve the user much more directly. Examples of Web 2.0 include social networking sites such as Facebook and Twitter (more on which below), collaborative media such as wikis, and hosting-services which allow users to upload their own content and share it with others, such as YouTube.

This online landscape is changing very quickly. There has been a feeling that libraries do not belong in this world, and that users do not wish to interact with libraries via these platforms. There may well have been a time when this was true – certainly many libraries in the early days of Web 2.0 (the early-to-mid noughties) were prone to letting the tail wag the dog, and setting up a MySpace site for their organization first, and trying to work out exactly what to do with it second. But things are changing. The way in which users consume and create content online has evolved, and 'social media' is no longer just a facilitator for 'social' interaction – it drives business, commerce and now learning, too.

For libraries, Web 2.0 and its applications are a way of connecting with new users, supporting existing users, and marketing their services to pertinent demographics.

Blogs

Blogs and *blog* are a shortening of 'weblogs', the original term used to describe websites which featured new content on a regular basis, usually displayed in reverse chronological order with the newest at the top. The key thing that defines a blog is the fact it has regular entries (usually text, but often pictures or videos too) – most blogs are also interactive in that they allow the user to subscribe to them so they receive each new entry, and to comment on them. Blogging is hugely popular – at the time of writing there are over 178 million publicly available blogs, with over 94,000 new ones being registered every 24 hours (see http://blog.nielsen.com/nielsenwire/social/ for up-to-date statistics).

Blog is also a verb – 'to blog' is write a blog or blog post about something. In the library context, blogs are used to update users and potential users on new collections, new technologies, building work and all sorts of other developments. Their strength as a marketing tool lies in the fact that they allow interaction, they can be less formal in style than many other library communications, and, as the user can subscribe, they then become something of a captive audience to which to market.

Comments can be left on blogs by anyone online – in general commenting should be encouraged, as it can lead to useful interaction with users. Libraries can control the comments – on most blogging platforms, comments will be queued, awaiting moderation by the blog's administrator (you): you can approve them so they appear on the blog itself, or not if they contain content you are uncomfortable with. In order to avoid sorting through hundreds of irrelevant *spam* comments that aren't from real people, a *spam filter* is always worth using to ensure automated advertising (usually of unseemly content!) doesn't appear on your library blog.

Wordpress (www.wordpress.com), *Tyepad* (www.typepad.com) and *Blogger* (www.blogger.com) are all examples of platforms which facilitate blogging.

Thousands of library blogs exist. For examples, see http://uklibraryblogs.pbworks.com for a list of UK library and librarian blogs.

Microblogs and short-form blogs

Microblogging features regularly updated content in the same way as standard blogging, but with much reduced size – usually one or two sentences, or just a single picture or video. The most common examples of microblogs are Twitter (www.twitter.com) and FriendFeed (www.friendfeed.com). Of these, Twitter is the most popular and the most used by libraries.

Twitter: on this platform each entry is described as a *tweet* (and the act described as *tweeting*) and must be 140 characters or less, including spaces. There is an oft-expressed sentiment among people who don't use Twitter that 'you can't say anything in 140 characters' – this is surprisingly not the case. Users follow each other on Twitter – in their 'timeline' they will see the majority of tweets from those they follow (the exception being tweets which are addressed to someone else whom the user does *not* follow, in which case these won't appear in the user's timeline).

Retweeting: if someone *retweets* or *RTs* a tweet, this allows more people to see it. For example, if you followed me on Twitter, and I retweeted something from my local library, you'd see this tweet whether or not you follow my local library. As such, for a library to have their tweets RT'd is very much a good thing, exposing the content to new audiences.

Libraries find Twitter to be a particularly useful tool for marketing because users will reply to tweets and generally interact and converse with the library, leading to valuable insights and the development of relationships.

Short-form blogs sit somewhere between a regular blog and a microblog. Tumblr (www.tumblr.com) is the most common example of this. At the time of writing it is the fastest growing social media platform.

Social networks

In the sense in which it is used in this book, *social network* refers to online platforms that bring together people or organizations and connect them through common interests.

Facebook (www.facebook.com) is of course the most famous example and is far and away the most popular social network on the internet – in fact, at the time of writing it's the most popular *site* on the internet (more frequently used even than Google). Facebook has over 800 million *active* users – the total number of people with accounts is close to one seventh of the world's population. Businesses see Facebook as essential to their marketing efforts, not least because the site has evolved beyond its original intention to connect people socially and become a destination for people seeking information, via their network of peers. See up-to-date statistics on Facebook at http://newsroom.fb.com/content/default.aspx?NewsAreaId=22.

LinkedIn (www.linkedin.com) is described as a *professional network*, in that its primary purpose is job- and career-related. However, the division between 'personal' and 'professional' networks has blurred in recent years, and most people use their social networks for both.

Twitter is an example of a social network, as well as being an example of a microblog, because it connects people online.

Other tools

Other Web 2.0 tools, such as geolocational apps, are defined in Chapter 7. This Appendix also has a corresponding web page with more information, at **www.librarymarketingtoolkit.com/p/web-20-glossary.html**. The page includes a comments box for requesting definitions of any tools not covered in the text here.

References

Abram, S. (2011a) *Discussion on Marketing and Libraries*, personal communication, 14 June 2011.

Abram, S. (2011b) LMD Marketing Breakfast panel session. In *SLA Annual Conference 2011*. Philadelphia, USA, 11–15 June 2011.

Bates, M. E. (2011) Creating Groupies: info-pro guerrilla marketing. In *SLA Annual Conference 2011*. Philadelphia, USA, 11–15 June 2011.

Batts, S. (2011) SLA Rising Stars. In *SLA Annual Conference 2011*. Philadelphia, USA, 11–15 June 2011.

Booms, B. H. and Bitner, M. J. (1981), Marketing Strategies and Organization Structures for Service Firms. In Donnelly, J. H. and George, W. R. (eds), *Marketing of Services*, American Marketing Association, Chicago, IL, 47–51.

Bridges, W. (2009) *Managing Transitions: Making the most of change*, 3rd edn, Nicholas Brealey Publishing.

CIPFA (2010) Children's Fiction is a Major Growth Area for Libraries, *Chartered Institute of Public Finance and Accountancy Press Releases*, 12 May, www.cipfa.org.uk/press/press_show.cfm?news_id=60897.

Clark, I. (2010) The Media and the Public Library Narrative, *Thoughts of a Wannabe Librarian*, 24 August, http://thoughtsofawannabelibrarian.wordpress.com/2010/08/24/the-media-and-the-public-library-narrative/.

Court, D. et al. (2010) The Consumer Decision Journey, *McKinsey Quarterly*, www.mckinseyquarterly.com/The_consumer_decision_journey_2373.

Dao, F. (2006) Marketing Your Mission Statement, *Inc.com*, www.inc.com/resources/leadership/articles/20061101/dao.html.

Dowd, N. et al. (2010) Word-of-Mouth Marketing. In Dowd, N., Evangeliste, M. and Silberman, J., *Bite-Sized Marketing*, London, Facet Publishing, 11.

Esteve-Coll, E. (1985) Marketing the Academic Library, *Information and Library Manager*, **5** (3).

Exact Target (2011) *Report #4: Twitter X-Factors,*
www.exacttarget.com/subscribers-fans-followers/twitter-x-factors.aspx.

Feddern, D. (2011a) Getting Started with Search Engine Optimization (SEO): Step
One, *Techsoup for libraries,* www.techsoupforlibraries.org/blog/getting-started-
with-search-engine-optimization-seo-step-one.

Feddern, D. (2011b) 5 Keywords Libraries Should Own on Google, *SEO for Libraries,*
http://seoforlibraries.com/seoblog/2011/05/20/5-keywords-libraries-should-own-
on-google.

GlobalWebIndex (2011) Global Map of Social Networking 2011,
http://visual.ly/global-map-social-networking-2011.

Hennah, K. (2005) Image Handbook: Public Libraries, Australia: State Library of
Victoria.

Holley, R. (2010) Crowdsourcing: how and why should libraries do it?, *DLib,* **16** (3),
www.dlib.org/dlib/march10/holley/03holley.html.

Information Commissioner's Office (2011) *Data protection principles,*
www.ico.gov.uk/for_organisations/data_protection/the_guide/
the_principles.aspx.

Kendrick, T. (2006) *Developing Strategic Marketing Plans that Really Work: a toolkit for
public libraries,* Facet Publishing.

King, D. L. (2008) Designing the Digital Experience: how to use experience design
tools and techniques to build web sites customers love, Cyberage Publishing.

Koster, L. (2010) Do we Need Mobile Library Services?,
http://commonplace.net/2010/12/do-we-need-mobile-library-services.

Macale, S. (2011) Twitter Users are More Likely to Impact Your Brand than any
Other Social Network, http://thenextweb.com/twitter/2011/08/18/twitter-users-are-
more-likely-to-impact-your-brand-than-any-other-social-network.

McCarthy Madsen, C. (2009) The Importance of Marketing Digital Collections:
including a case study from Harvard's Open Collections Program, *ALISS
Quarterly,* **5** (1), 2–9.

MLA (2010) *Public's Wishes Revealed,*
www.mla.gov.uk/news_and_views/press_releases/2010/ipsosmori.

OCLC (2006) *College Students' Perceptions of Libraries and Information Resources,* OCLC
Reports, www.oclc.org/reports/perceptionscollege.htm.

Pouros, A. (2011) *Social Proof for Digital Marketers: a primer,*
http://econsultancy.com/uk/blog/7224-social-proof-for-digimarketers-a-primer.

PRWeb (2010) Boopsie: Non-catalog services more popular with mobile library
patrons, www.prweb.com/releases/2010/11/prweb4787284.htm.

Rafiq, M. and Ahmed, P. (1995) Using the 7 Ps as a Generic Marketing Mix: an exploratory survey of UK and European marketing academics, *Marketing Intelligence and Planning*, **13** (9), 4–15.

Skinner, F. (2010a) Sorry, the Demise of the Library is Well Overdue, *The Times* (27 August).

Skinner, F. (2010b) Why I'm on a New Page with Local Libraries: it was my ideas that were dog-eared, not the places themselves, *The Times* (1 October).

SLA (2011) Alignment Project, www.sla.org/content/SLA/alignment/index.cfm.

Tay, A. (2011) *Comparison of 40 Mobile Library Sites*, http://musingsaboutlibrarianship.blogspot.com/2010/04/comparison-of-40-mobile-library-sites.html.

Tay, A. and Travis, T. (2011) Designing Low-Cost Mobile Websites for Libraries, *Bulletin of American Society for Information Science and Technology*, **38** (1), www.asis.org/Bulletin/Oct-11/OctNov11Travis_Tay.pdf.

TNS (2010) *TNS Digital Life October 2010*, http://2010.tnsdigitallife.com.

Index